EASY

one-bowl
baking

EASY
one-bowl
baking

NO-FUSS RECIPES
FOR SWEET AND SAVORY
BAKED GOODS

Kelli Marks

Photography by Marija Vidal

ROCKRIDGE
PRESS

For general information on our other products and services or to obtain technical support, please contact our Customer Care Department within the United States at (866) 744-2665, or outside the United States at (510) 253-0500.

Rockridge Press publishes its books in a variety of electronic and print formats. Some content that appears in print may not be available in electronic books, and vice versa.

Interior and Cover Designer: Linda Snorina
Art Producer: Hannah Dickerson
Editor: Cecily McAndrews
Production Editor: Ruth Sakata Corley
Production Manager: Jose Olivera

Photography © 2021 Marija Vidal, food styling by Victoria Woollard
Author photo courtesy of Kyle G. McLaughlin

Cover: Lime-Raspberry Pie, page 81.

ISBN: Print 978-1-63807-900-2
       eBook 978-1-63807-970-5

R0

To **Erin**, my recipe bouncer-offer,
Katie, my eternal cheerleader,
and **Brad**, my never-ending
dishwasher and taste-tester.

Contents

Introduction ix

Chapter 4: CAKES AND CUPCAKES 57

Chapter 5: COBBLERS, PUDDINGS, AND FRUITY DESSERTS 79

Chapter 6: YEASTED BREADS AND SAVORY BAKES 93

Introduction

If I want you to know that you're special, I will bake for you.

I got into cake decorating when my grandparents had their 50th wedding anniversary. I thought it would be special if I made the cake for their party. I taught myself how to bake from a cookbook and eventually created a four-tier cake completely from scratch. I was absolutely hooked.

After that cake for my grandparents, I continued practicing and eventually opened my own bakery. We sold all the typical fare you would expect in a place dedicated to sugar: cupcakes, brownies, French macarons, cakes, and pies. Eventually I decided that my adorable bakery was more than I could handle. My career path meandered after that, including co-owning a restaurant, working as a pastry chef at the William J. Clinton Presidential Center and Library, operating a ghost bakery from a warehouse, teaching baking at a technical college, and eventually operating a cottage bakery specializing in wedding cakes.

There's a saying: "Once you know the rules, then you can break them." I spent the time learning the rules; now I'm cutting the corners, but not the quality. And while it's not unusual for me to spend days creating something really special, I don't always have that kind of time to invest in a baked good. There are times you realize that a new neighbor has joined the community, a family member is popping in from out of town, or you just *need* some sugar quickly. That's what these recipes are all about.

In my house, I do all the baking and my husband does all the cleaning, and while he loves the desserts I make, he does not love the mess. Enter one-bowl baking. The majority of these recipes are mixed in a single bowl and then baked in another pan. After all is said and done, all there is to wash is one bowl, one mixing utensil, usually one measuring cup, and then some sort of baking pan. No sink full of dishes! And at the end, I have something beautiful, flavorful, and full of love to share.

Whether you picked up this book because the cover was cute, because you have always said "I can't bake; it's too hard," or because you already know your way around the kitchen and you just wanted a fresh take, welcome! I've packed this book with a variety of flavors and techniques, including everything from cookies and quick breads to cakes and even a few yeasted breads and savory bakes. Grab your favorite bowl and a whisk and get ready to learn my best one-bowl baking secrets. I've got some things to show you.

Chapter 1

One-Bowl Baking Essentials

You might feel the urge to skip over this chapter, but don't. Here I outline the tools you will need for one-bowl baking success, the ingredients you will use most often, and some of the motivation behind why I bake and how these recipes came about. Can baking be easy? Less daunting? Less messy? But still flavorful and fun? Yes. Let me show you how.

Butter Pecan–Dulce de Leche Coffee Cake
page 66

Welcome to Easy, Mess-Free Baking

One-bowl baking is just that: Every recipe in this book uses one bowl to mix everything and then it's transferred to a baking vessel—what it's baked in. I tried to stick to some simple, standard pans in most of these recipes: a loaf pan, muffin tins, an 8-inch square baking pan, a 9-by-13-inch baking pan, a Bundt pan, and, of course, a few baking sheets. I recommend having at least two baking sheets so you can be ready to pop the next batch of cookies in as soon as the first ones come out. And just for fun, I even have a recipe that is baked in the bowl—check out my Baked Alaska Bowl (page 74).

Speaking of bowls, I used two types of mixing bowls for these recipes. When I call for a medium bowl, I use a 3-quart bowl. And when I call for a large bowl, I use a 5-quart bowl. Typically that larger bowl is used for yeasted doughs to allow space for the bread dough to proof and double in size.

The recipes in this book are quick bakes. Most go from start to cooling time in under an hour. After that hour, you'll have a delicious, made-from-scratch dessert without needing to clean your kitchen from top to bottom. I've used my years of training to develop simple recipes that take out all the unnecessary steps. I pack in flavor and only use a few premade ingredients where absolutely necessary.

Culinary school teaches students the art of mise en place, which is French for "everything in its place." Mise en place refers to the act of getting all your ingredients ready and measured before you start. I love it because you will never accidentally leave out an ingredient, as can happen when you grab and measure as you mix. It helps prevent you from missing steps, and it keeps you organized in the kitchen. However, you do end up with lots of dirty bowls and measuring spoons and cups. To really work with the simplicity of one-bowl baking, I developed a type of reverse mise en place system that keeps me from dirtying unnecessary bowls while still keeping the ingredients I need organized. I pull out all my ingredients, measure what I need as the recipe calls for it, and put it away immediately. That way I still never forget an ingredient, but I clean and stay organized as I go.

THE BEST ONE-BOWL BAKES

I'm not going to lie, I have some complicated recipes, like a cheesecake that requires three whole bowls to make, but that's not what this book is about. Instead, I simplified that recipe and created a unique Cheesecake Napoleon (page 84). Everyone loves pumpkin bread, but have you ever tried Sweet Potato Bread (page 49)? It's a different take on something familiar. Of course, there are the classics, too, like Zucchini-Apple Bread (page 52), Russian Tea Cakes (page 25), and some of the best Big Ol' Biscuits (page 50) you'll ever find, if I do say so myself. These recipes offer a great start to the day, a strong finish for dinner, and, of course, more desserts than you can shake a stick at. And all it takes is just one bowl.

WHAT WORKS FOR ONE-BOWL BAKING?

When you try to skip steps or adjust them, it's important to know what those steps do. When butter is creamed, it creates little air bubbles, which make your baked good lighter. When butter is melted, those air bubbles are lost, resulting in a denser cake and crispier cookie edges. So the question becomes: When can we use those qualities to our advantage? Certain quick breads start simply with oil. By replacing the oil with butter, we are able to mix easily but still have that buttery flavor. And the fact is, some recipes—think cookies and muffins—are better suited for one-bowl baking.

ONE-BOWL BAKING, STEP-BY-STEP

One-bowl baking relies on efficiency. If I need to melt butter for a recipe, I try to start with the butter in the actual bowl that I'm going to use for mixing. Boom! That's already one less bowl to have to wash. Or, I will reuse a utensil multiple times. If I need to melt butter and then later measure milk, I will melt my butter in my liquid measuring cup, add it to the bowl, and then pour the milk into the measuring cup. It's not rocket science, and I'm sure you already do tons of these little hacks already.

A typical baking recipe begins with creaming the butter and sugar, followed by any stabilizers (leaveners, sour cream, eggs, and such), then finishes with liquids and dry ingredients. Larger recipes will have the last two components added in alternating batches.

For yeast-risen recipes, I traditionally bloom the yeast in a separate bowl and add it later. For one-bowl baking, I'm blooming the yeast in the mixing bowl and working off that. (Honestly, I think I'm going to do that every time from now on.)

HACKS TO MAKE (ALMOST) ANY RECIPE ONE-BOWL

When I worked at my ghost bakery, I was in the back corner of a large ware-house. When I needed to wash anything I had to walk super far away, so I started getting really creative with trying to use as few dishes as possible (and not cross-contaminate). Here are some things I gleaned from that experience.

Put all your liquids into one large measuring cup—milk, oil, eggs, and even sour cream get poured into a single place. Use liquid displacement to measure things like sour cream. For example, if you have 1 cup of milk and need ½ cup of sour cream, add sour cream to the milk until the overall measurement is 1½ cups.

If you have a topping that's going to be baked, scrape the batter out of your mixing bowl with a spatula, then just mix the topping in that same bowl without rinsing. If a little muffin batter gets mixed into your crumble, there's very little harm, if any, and no compromise to the flavor.

A secret: I never sift flour. If you have your whisk out, run it through the flour. This aerates the flour to get rid of any lumps, and it's kind of soothing. If you don't have a whisk, you can do the same thing by lightly scooping and dropping repeatedly with your measuring cup. When you go to finally scoop your flour to measure it, do so gently (don't pack it) and scrape the top level with the back of a butter knife or spatula for an even measure.

The microwave is the one-bowl baker's best friend. Use it to soften butter and cream cheese or melt chocolate. Just make sure you're working with a microwave-safe bowl.

The Digital Food Scale: A Baking MVP

When I learned how to bake, I measured ingredients only by volume and I was scared to try weight measurements. What do those numbers even mean? Isn't a scale expensive? It just seemed scary. But it's not. I grabbed a decent electric scale for around $10. My advice is to choose a scale with a removable top for easy cleaning and, if you can find it, one where the screen pulls out so it's easier to read when using a large bowl.

Weight measurements are easier and much more precise than volume measurements. You don't have to use measuring cups, so that's even fewer things to wash. The important thing to remember is to tare the scale so that you're not measuring the weight of the bowl. Taring means zeroing out the weight so that the scale pretends there's nothing on it, leaving only the weight of the next ingredient. To do this, place the bowl on the scale and press the tare button until it reads 0. Then add your first ingredient, up to the weight you need, and tare again to 0 before adding the next ingredient.

Essential Baking Equipment

It's tool time! I love to try new kitchen gear; all those one-trick gadgets that people love to dunk on are my favorite. But honestly, I can do without most of them and so can you. Below are the tools I find absolutely necessary—and a few that make baking easier, but aren't essential.

PYREX OR CERAMIC BOWL: I have several stainless-steel bowls, and while they are great for cleaning and nesting uniformly, they do have a major downfall—they can't be used in the microwave. For one-bowl baking, a Pyrex or ceramic bowl is best. Make sure that it's labeled safe for microwave use; I have an adorable plastic bowl that gets very hot if microwaved. You can pick up a Pyrex or ceramic bowl for $10 to $15.

PYREX MEASURING CUP: I recommend finding a measuring cup that's either Pyrex or plastic—I have one that has angled measurements both inside and outside that I love. Aim for something that will hold between 2 and 4 cups, so that you can use it for everything. Make sure they are microwave safe, too.

MEASURING SPOONS AND CUPS: I have two sets of measuring spoons: one set for liquids and one for dry ingredients. This keeps me from going back and forth and having to wash each time. (Confession time: When it comes to leaveners and salt, I never wash my spoons.) Depending on how fancy you are, you can spend $5 or up to $20 for a set.

WHISK: Whisks come in a variety of sizes and designs. I have a large balloon whisk that is stainless steel, but the one I go back to time and time again is my OXO whisk, which only cost $10. It's a smaller, more compact whisk with a silicone handle that's easier to work with.

SILICONE SPATULA: I have several spatulas, and choose which one to use depending on what I'm baking. For the most part, I want something with a big paddle head for mixing and a good angle to scrape every bit out of the bowl. No use wasting any deliciousness! You can buy sets for around $10. If you're going to be working with a lot of cakes, an offset spatula (also called an angled spatula) will make your life easier.

BAKING SCALE: A digital baking scale eliminates the need to use multiple measuring cups and makes sure that your baking is precise. (Check out the Digital Food Scale: A Baking MVP box on page 5 for more information.) Grab one for $10 to $20.

RIMMED BAKING SHEETS: Also known as a sheet pan, a baking sheet is like a cookie sheet with a lip around the edge. I move quickly in the kitchen, and the chance of me slinging a cookie off a flat cookie sheet is high, so I tend to stick to the rimmed models. A restaurant supply company is your best bet for baking sheets of various sizes. The smallest can start at only $3, with most topping out at $10.

CAKE AND BROWNIE PANS: I use a few different cake pans throughout this book: 8-inch square, 8-inch round, and 9-by-13-inch rectangle. If you're just starting out baking, these are great staples to get you started. I prefer using metal pans, because glass is slower to heat up and then retains heat longer. I recommend using only metal for the recipes in this book so that the bake times will be accurate. These pans can be purchased for around $7 to $12 each.

BUNDT OR TUBE PAN: Bundt pans come in a variety of beautiful designs. I have a few different ones, but the more intricate designs have a tendency to leave stuck-on bits when you're removing the cake from the pan. If you're just starting out, I suggest sticking to the basic Bundt pan and work your way up as you gain confidence. A simple Bundt starts at $10. If you make the Strawberry Angel Shortcake (page 76), it must be done in a tube pan. While it looks similar to a Bundt pan, it has a slightly different shape. I picked up a tube pan recently for $16.

LOAF PAN: Did you know that loaf pans come in different sizes? I didn't at first. I have a smaller 8-inch pan that is great for my quick breads, while my pound cake recipe really needs a larger 10-by-5-inch loaf pan. You can purchase a smaller loaf pan for under $10.

MUFFIN TINS: For muffins, cupcakes, and mini cheesecakes, muffin tins are a kitchen workhorse. Don't forget to get some paper liners to keep your baked goods fresher and keep your pans cleaner. There are cute silicone muffin tins, but they have so much flex that you need to place them on a sheet pan so I stick to metal tins. You can get a set of two standard-size muffin tins for around $12.

HAND MIXER: Is it impossible to cream butter or whip egg whites by hand? No, but a hand mixer will cut your prep time down drastically. And they really don't break the bank—you can get one that includes several attachments, including a dough hook, for around $30.

PARCHMENT PAPER: I (big puffy pink heart) love parchment paper. It makes cleanup easy, you can cut it to any size needed, and the overall cost is low. If you can find precut sheets, I recommend investing in them.

FOOD PROCESSOR: A food processor is an investment for sure, but it makes dreamy shortbread cookies and chops nuts like you wouldn't believe. If you are baking for someone who has a wheat allergy and find yourself needing nut flours, a food processor will pay for itself in no time because you can grind the nuts yourself.

PIZZA CUTTER: I love my pizza cutter. Some people think it's a one-food-use tool, but these folks are just not using their imagination. I use mine constantly, to cut yeasted doughs, fondant, and—yep—pizza.

Do I Need a Stand Mixer?

I have a not-so-healthy love affair with my stand mixers. Yes, mixers, plural. I have the pretty one that sits on my counter, a large commercial unit I use when I make big batches, another one just for photos and as a backup when needed, and then my tried-and-true workhorse mixer that has seen me through thick and thin (batters).

So am I a fan? Of course. Do I have a problem? Probably. Stand mixers are great for thick doughs, fluffy creamed butter, or any recipe that requires a long mixing time. Plus, I love how it's hands-free: I can collect other ingredients or turn on my oven while it does the work. But I wanted to make these recipes approachable, so every recipe in this book can be mixed either by hand (whisk or spatula) or with a hand mixer (helpful for the beefier recipes). Can you dump these things into a stand mixer and let it do the work? Absolutely, but it's not required.

Ingredients

These are the building blocks of almost all baked goods. This list doesn't include every ingredient you might ever use when you bake, but it will do the trick for most recipes.

FLOUR

When I started baking I had no idea that there were different kinds of flours, and no, I don't mean brands. For traditional white (wheat) flours, the primary difference is the protein content. Going from most protein to least, the list runs bread flour > all-purpose flour > pastry flour > cake flour. **Bread flour** has the most protein, and therefore more gluten, which gives your breads a chewier texture. If a recipe calls for bread flour, it needs the sturdiness. **Cake flour** has the least protein and gives cakes a soft crumb. The goal in using it is to have a light and soft baked good. There are a few recipes in this book that call for cake flour and bread flour; in these cases it will be fine to substitute with **all-purpose flour**, if that's what you have, but I would not recommend substituting bread flour for cake flour or vice versa.

Additionally, there are alternative flours, such as **almond flour** (also called almond meal), **whole-wheat flour**, **buckwheat flour**, **rice flour**, and even **potato flour**. While all the alternatives flours except whole-wheat have the benefit of being gluten-free, I tend to stick to almond flour as my most used alternative flour, thanks to the additional flavor it provides. These alternative flours cannot be simply swapped out to make a recipe gluten-free, so if that is your goal, find a one-for-one gluten-free flour—I like Bob's Red Mill.

SUGAR

Sugar plays a pivotal role in most baked goods. It's responsible for adding sweetness, of course, but sugar also contributes structure, depth of flavor, moisture, and, in some instances, crunch. There are several types of sugar used throughout this book. **Granulated sugar** is your basic white sugar. **Powdered sugar** (aka confectioners' sugar) is sugar that has been ground even finer and has a bit of cornstarch in it to prevent it from caking, making it perfect for situations where you need a sweetener that dissolves quickly. **Light brown sugar** is granulated sugar with the addition of molasses, and **dark brown sugar** is (you guessed it) granulated sugar with even more molasses—twice as much, to be exact. If a recipe specifically calls for light or dark brown sugar and you have only the other kind on hand, that's fine. And if you've run out, you can make light brown sugar by adding 1 tablespoon of molasses to 1 cup of granulated sugar, or 2 tablespoons to make dark brown sugar.

Here is where the fun sugars come in: **Turbinado**, **demerara**, and **sanding sugar** are all larger-grain sugars that are great to add crunch to the tops of desserts because the grains won't melt from the heat of the oven. I call for demerara sugar a few times in this book, but you can use either of the other types instead.

Honey is another sweetener used in my recipes. Because it is liquid, it cannot be used interchangeably with sugar.

LEAVENERS

Leaveners add lift and airiness to baked goods. There are a few different kinds, and each has a different quality. **Baking soda** requires an acid and a liquid to activate it and is more powerful than baking powder, so I tend to use less of it. **Baking powder** contains its own acid and requires only a liquid to activate it. It's also often double-acting, meaning that the first reaction happens when it becomes wet and the second reaction happens when it's heated. Both baking soda and baking powder have an average shelf life of 6 months to a year, so check the expiration date on the package. These are typically used in cookies, quick breads, muffins, and scones.

Yeast is most often used in bread recipes. My grandmother has always said that yeast is like people: It needs a warm place and something sweet to eat to be happy. There are two main types: instant yeast, which can be folded right into a recipe, and active dry yeast, which needs to be "woken up" with warm water and sugar. Healthy yeast bubbles and foams when introduced to warm water and sugar. If your yeast is stale, no reaction will occur. I buy my yeast in bulk and store it in the freezer to keep it fresh. My kitchen always seems to be cold, so I often use my oven as a proofer. I heat it to the lowest temp (170°F for me), then turn it off (you want it warm but not *too* warm; if it's too hot, it will kill the yeast) and place the dough in the warm oven. Feel free to use this trick with any yeasted recipe.

BUTTER AND OIL

When it comes to fats, in my book, **butter** is best. I love the flavor and richness it imparts. Butter is versatile: I love to grate cold butter for perfect bits in my scones and biscuits, whip room-temperature butter for cakes and cookies, and melt butter for brownies. While technically you can swap margarine for butter, margarine has less flavor and won't do the recipe justice. When I know that I have a lot of baking on the agenda, I set my butter out on the counter to come to room temperature, often the night before. My grandmother always had at least one stick in her CorningWare butter dish on the counter.

If you don't realize the baking bug is about to bite and your butter is still rock-hard, a few seconds in the microwave can help it along greatly, but keep a close watch: You want it softened, not in puddles. Also, a big block of butter takes longer to soften than several small pieces. I cut the butter into tablespoon pieces and let it hang out while I gather the rest of my ingredients. It also helps to move it to a warm place in your kitchen, like near or on top of a preheating oven.

Sometimes I use vegetable oil in my recipes. I prefer canola oil, as it has a light flavor. What oil lacks in flavor, it makes up for by adding texture, moisture, and tenderness to your bakes. If you would like to cut out a few calories, you can substitute applesauce for all or part of the oil in a recipe. Substitute applesauce for butter only in recipes where the butter is melted.

One-Bowl Baking with Kids

Every great chef needs a sous-chef, and kids are great at this. One-bowl baking is a fantastic way to introduce kids to cooking. It helps them feel comfortable in the kitchen, teaches them about food, and allows them to play safely (since the oven portion can be done by an adult). The majority of these recipes are quick, easy, and foolproof, so you don't have to worry about the kids losing interest or being confused. Baking is a great opportunity to teach things like fractions; even some adults think that ¼ is more than ⅓.

Certain tasks work better for younger kids (ages 5 to 9), while other tasks can be done by older kids (ages 10 and up). Younger kids can measure out leaveners or liquids and can drop cookies onto baking sheets. They can also do a lot of the tasks that aren't specifically baking, like putting the paper liners in a muffin pan or using the pan spray. Kids love to be the Head Sprinkle Engineer. Older kids can be in charge of mixing, setting timers, gathering ingredients, cracking eggs, and watching for doneness.

Whatever tasks they accomplish, you know they'll bake up some delicious memories.

CHOCOLATE AND COCOA POWDER

Chocolate comes in a variety of forms: bars, wafers, chips, and even blocks. Each one has benefits and best uses. Chocolate chips are obviously great for cookies, but they have added stabilizers to help them keep their shape, so they might not melt as well. Larger bars and blocks are best for cakes and puddings. Wafers are designed to melt quickly, so they're best for things like ganache. I recommend working with the best-quality chocolate you can find; my favorites are Callebaut and Guittard. These brands aren't always available where I live, so I work with the best I can find, usually Ghirardelli chips.

The majority of my recipes use **semisweet**, **bittersweet**, or **dark chocolate**. If you're a fan of **milk chocolate**, the finished product might be a tiny bit sweeter, but it should still work. The amount of cocoa in chocolate determines how sweet it is. Semisweet is around 60 percent cocoa, bittersweet is usually around 70 percent, and dark chocolate is anything above 70 percent. **White chocolate** isn't technically chocolate since it doesn't have any chocolate solids, and it can be quite sweet. When used judiciously, white chocolate adds a lovely sweet, creamy flavor.

Hershey's unsweetened **natural cocoa powder** is my usual go-to, but I have a few recipes that need the smoother flavor and deeper color of **Dutch-process cocoa powder**. Do not substitute one for the other, as it can mess up the leavening.

DAIRY PRODUCTS

Dairy products add richness, flavor, and moisture to baked goods.

CREAM: When a recipe calls for cream, it's usually to add richness and, in some cases, airiness. Cream can be whipped to add volume in a way that can't be done with milk. Heavy cream (often labeled "heavy whipping cream" at the supermarket) has at least 36 percent fat, whereas whipping cream has around 30 percent. Heavy cream gives a sturdier hold in things like whipped cream, while whipping cream will have a softer peak. Either will work fine in most recipes.

CREAM CHEESE: Cream cheese is like sour cream on steroids (in the very best way). It adds richness and a tangy flavor but also has the benefit of being stable enough to be the base for things like cheesecake and frosting. In an absolute pinch, it can be substituted for heavy cream at a one-to-one ratio.

MILK: I use whole milk in my recipes, but you can definitely use 2 percent. The batter will be a bit less thick, which typically isn't a problem in most baked goods, but it can change the texture of custards. I love almond milk and always put it in my coffee. It's a great option for anyone who has a problem with dairy (but obviously not for anyone with nut allergies). Soy milk is the closest replacement for whole milk, as it is high in protein and has a similar flavor. I avoid alternative milks when I'm baking for others since I don't always know of any dietary restrictions they may have, but if you're baking for yourself, I encourage you to use your favorite.

SOUR CREAM: Anytime I think a recipe is missing something, I reach for sour cream to increase the richness and moisture. Sour cream also imparts a tanginess that brings balance to baked goods.

YOGURT: Yogurt serves a similar function as sour cream; in fact, I often substitute these on a one-for-one basis. One nice thing about yogurt is that it's available in a number of flavors, giving you the option to layer flavors in your baking. For instance, I use honey-flavored yogurt in my Honey-Walnut Muffins (page 46).

SPICES AND PANTRY STAPLES

I like to have a well-stocked pantry, because most of these staples stay good for a long time and you never know when the urge to bake will strike! Here are some of the items I always have on hand for baking.

ASSORTED NUTS: I am a huge fan of texture, and nuts are a great way to add crunch and flavor to desserts. Pecans have a light sweetness. Almonds have a clean, almost neutral flavor, and cashews are buttery and rich. These can also be ground to create gluten-free flours.

CINNAMON: One of the most basic seasonings, ground cinnamon can add a layer of flavor to just about any other flavor. In my cherry Cheesecake Napoleon (page 84), it might seem unusual, but it adds a warmth that would be lacking otherwise.

CORNSTARCH: Cornstarch has a few uses in baking. For instance, I keep it on hand to prevent fondant from sticking to the counter when I roll it out. But its real powerhouse use is to thicken things like curds, fruit purees, and custards. To use it without leaving lumps, make a slurry by whisking together cornstarch and cold water until smooth, then add the slurry to the mixture in the bowl.

NONSTICK SPRAY: When I bake cakes, I always line my pans with parchment paper, but I also give the paper a generous coating of nonstick cooking spray as extra insurance. There's nothing more frustrating than baking a beautiful cake that won't come out of the pan. I've also been known to spray some baked goods if I need a topping to stick.

NUTMEG: This is another versatile spice. I suggest buying whole nutmeg seeds and grating your own for a fresher flavor. Nutmeg provides an earthiness and really adds oomph to many warm, spicy desserts. I also love cardamom for this same reason.

OATS: Several of my desserts use old-fashioned rolled oats. They add bulk to baked goods, and they can be used as-is, ground into a type of flour, or even made into a milk. Oh, and they're gluten-free (just be sure to look for oats marked gluten-free, as sometimes they're cross-contaminated with gluten-containing products at the factory). Talk about a versatile ingredient!

SALT: When I cook, I prefer kosher salt, because the larger grains provide a satisfying pop of saltiness. But when it comes to baking, I prefer to use standard table salt, because the smaller grains incorporate more easily into batters, and they have a better chance of dissolving in nonbaked items like frostings and fillings. I keep flaky Maldon salt on hand as a finishing salt; the large crystals are crunchy and elegant.

VANILLA EXTRACT: This one might feel like a no-brainer—it's a standard in so many baked goods. If you spring for real vanilla, you'll typically find varieties from Tahiti and Madagascar. I find that Tahitian has stronger floral notes, while Madagascar vanilla has a richer, creamier flavor. However, vanilla is very expensive right now, so I tend to save the real stuff for desserts where the vanilla flavor really needs to shine. If I'm just using it to round out other flavors, I often use imitation vanilla extract because it's less noticeable.

VINEGAR: Vinegar always has a place in my pantry, and I tend to keep a variety on hand. Apple cider vinegar has fruity undertones, making it great for baking. When I'm all out of buttermilk, I add 1 tablespoon of white vinegar to 1 cup of whole milk.

One-Bowl Techniques

Since all of the recipes in this book are easy and quick, the methods used are all pretty simple, too. Here's a rundown of what you can expect to have to do in these recipes.

MIXING: This covers a multitude of actual tasks, such as stirring, beating, and blending. Basically, you're combining two or more ingredients until the batter or dough is homogeneous. You don't want to overmix, as this can make your baked goods tough. An easy recipe that features mixing is my Zucchini-Apple Bread (page 52).

CREAMING: Creaming combines room-temperature butter and sugar, incorporating air until they are evenly combined, light, and fluffy. Typically this is done with a hand mixer or stand mixer. The Chocolate Chunk Pound Cake (page 63) is a good example of a recipe that relies on creaming.

FOLDING: Folding typically takes place when you have something that has a lot of air in it, like egg whites, and you want to carefully incorporate the dry ingredients without losing all the air that has been whipped into the egg whites. A recipe that features folding is the Strawberry Angel Shortcake (page 76). To fold, use a silicone spatula and gently cut the spatula through the center of the batter and out to the edge of the bowl, pulling the egg whites up and over the dry ingredients, then turn the bowl and repeat. Stop when there are still just a few streaks of egg whites visible. If you overfold the batter, you risk deflating the egg whites.

CUTTING IN BUTTER: This technique is a way to distribute cold butter throughout a dough, which results in a flaky baked good. The goal is to end up with pea-size pieces of butter studding the dough. Cutting in butter is most often used in recipes for scones, biscuits, and piecrusts. You can use a pastry cutter, but I often just use a fork to achieve a similar result. My recipe for Strawberry Weekday Biscuits (page 42) requires cutting in butter.

LEAVENING AND PROOFING: Leavening is what gives your baked goods lift. This is often done chemically with baking soda or baking powder, or organically with yeast or eggs. When using yeast, the first step is to wake it up with a bit of sugar and warmth and the second step is proofing the dough. Proofing is the process of allowing your dough to rise, usually until it has doubled in size. It should rest in a warm spot for an hour or more, or for up to 8 hours in the refrigerator. When the dough has a lot of flavors, a quick rise works just fine, but I find that when you have very simple flavors, a longer proof is better because it allows the flavors to mature. An example of a quick proof is the crust for the Stuffed-Crust Pepperoni Pizza (page 100) and a longer proof is the Citrus-Cherry Milk Bread (page 110).

Is It Done Yet?

You've made a delicious dessert and it's in the oven, but a crucial question lingers: How will I know when it is ready? If you know what to look for, a baked good will usually tell you when it's done: Golden brown is the name of the game. Once you become more comfortable baking and have done it for a while, even your nose will tell you. I know when my chocolate cake is ready to come out because the kitchen takes on a deeply sweet scent that makes the air feel thick. Even if I don't have a timer set, I know that I have 2 minutes before that cake is burnt. Here are a few indicators that will let you know when it's time to pull that baked good:

Bread: When bread is ready, it will pull away from the edges of the pan. The top and edges will be golden brown and it will feel firm. If it's a large loaf and you're not certain, you can insert a knife into the center. If it comes out clean, you're good.

Cake: Cake will also pull away from the edges of the pan, and the top will be golden with a matte appearance. If it's shiny, that's moisture and it means the cake isn't quite done. You can also press the center gently: if it springs back, it's ready. If the cake stays indented, it probably need a few more minutes.

Cookies: Cookies will have a golden edge once baked. I usually remove cookies from the oven while the centers are still a tiny bit underbaked. Personally I love a soft center, and the cookies will continue to bake on the pan while they cool.

Pies: With a pie, you have two elements to consider: the crust and the filling. You want a golden-brown crust and a set center. If the two elements are not baking at the same rate, you can slow down the color on the crust by covering it with aluminum foil.

About the Recipes

The recipes in this book are grouped into chapters by type—cookies, muffins, cupcakes, breads, and more.

LABELS

The recipes have the following labels so you know which ones will work for you and the people you're baking for:

DAIRY-FREE: Dairy-free recipes don't use any butter, milk, cheese, or cream-based products.

GLUTEN-FREE: This means that no gluten-containing products are used in the recipe. Wheat flour is typically replaced with a nut flour or ground oats. (My Blood Orange–Ricotta Cake on page 72 is gluten-free, but you'd never know.)

NUT-FREE: These recipes do not use any peanut or tree nut products, including nuts, nut butters, or nut oils.

VEGAN: Desserts that are vegan do not use any animal products at all, including dairy products, eggs, or honey.

TIPS

Many of the recipes include tips to help you get the most out of your baking.

INGREDIENT TIP: Some recipes feature a unique item that might be a bit harder to find. This tip provides more information about it.

SUBSTITUTION TIP: This tip lets you know when there's an easy substitution, in case you're out of an ingredient or you need to swap out because of an allergen.

TECHNIQUE TIP: Here I'll clue you in on some helpful hints that will make your baking go smoother and easier.

VARIATION TIP: In this tip, I suggest some easy swaps that can give you a whole new take on a recipe.

Chapter 2

Cookies, Bars, and Brownies

There's something so comforting about a cookie. Served warm or at room temperature, with or without milk, there's always some kind of ritual involved with eating them. Do you enjoy nibbling them from the edges or pulling them apart? Whether making them for a party or celebration, for a friend, or just because your sweet tooth is aching, this assortment will answer all your cravings, and quickly.

Raspberry-Pistachio Thumbprints
page 21

Peanut Butter Blossoms

Makes 24 cookies

Prep time: 15 minutes   **Bake time:** 10 to 12 minutes per sheet

Peanut butter and chocolate are arguably one of the best flavor pairings. It's the center of many popular candies and (ta-da!) these cookies. Task kids with unwrapping the candies and pressing them in place. Taking only 30 minutes from start to finish, this flavorful treat will be ready to enjoy in no time.

8 tablespoons (1 stick, 113g) unsalted butter, at room temperature

¾ packed cup (160g) light brown sugar

¼ cup (49g) granulated sugar, plus more for rolling

1 large egg

1 cup (270g) creamy peanut butter

1 teaspoon vanilla extract

2 cups (240g) all-purpose flour

½ teaspoon salt

½ teaspoon baking soda

24 chocolate kiss candies

TECHNIQUE TIP: To measure the peanut butter easily, spray your measuring cup with nonstick cooking spray beforehand. The peanut butter will easily slide out into the bowl.

1. Place an oven rack in the center of the oven and preheat to 375°F. Line two rimmed baking sheets with parchment paper.

2. In a medium mixing bowl, using a hand mixer on medium-high speed, cream together the butter, brown sugar, and granulated sugar until pale and fluffy, 2 to 3 minutes.

3. Add the egg and mix to combine. Mix in the peanut butter and vanilla until smooth and creamy.

4. Stir in the flour, salt, and baking soda until well combined.

5. Roll the dough into 1-inch balls. Place some granulated sugar on a plate or in a shallow bowl and roll the balls in the sugar, coating all around. Place the balls on the baking sheets, about 2 inches apart.

6. Bake one sheet at a time for 10 to 12 minutes, until the cookies are lightly browned.

7. Immediately after removing the pan from the oven, gently press a chocolate kiss into the center of each cookie. Allow to cool completely.

SUBSTITUTION TIP: If peanuts are a problem, swap for another nut butter of your choice. Cashew butter is very good in this recipe.

Raspberry-Pistachio Thumbprints

Makes 24 cookies

Prep time: 10 minutes, plus 1 hour to chill   **Bake time:** 15 minutes per sheet

These soft, buttery cookies are a classic shortbread dough rolled in finely chopped pistachios. Then you simply make an indent with your thumb and fill it with jam. These cookies are pretty enough for a cookie tray for a friend but easy enough for a playtime tea date.

1 cup (2 sticks, 226g)
   unsalted butter, at room
   temperature
²/₃ cup (132g)
   granulated sugar
2 large egg yolks
2 teaspoons vanilla extract
1 teaspoon almond extract
2¼ cups (270g)
   all-purpose flour
1 teaspoon salt
1 cup (120g) shelled
   pistachios
3 tablespoons
   raspberry jam

TECHNIQUE TIP: If you're having trouble getting the pistachios to adhere to the cookie dough, roll the balls in lightly beaten egg white first.

1. In a medium bowl, using a hand mixer on medium-high speed, cream together the butter and sugar until pale and fluffy, 2 to 3 minutes.

2. Add the egg yolks, vanilla, and almond extract and mix until just combined, scraping down the sides of the bowl as needed. Add the flour and salt and mix until just combined.

3. Cover the bowl with plastic wrap and refrigerate the dough for 1 hour.

4. Place an oven rack in the center of the oven and preheat to 400°F. Line two rimmed baking sheets with parchment paper.

5. Put the pistachios in a heavy-duty, gallon-size resealable bag, press out the air, and seal. Use a rolling pin or the flat side of a wooden mallet, to smash them into very small pieces.

6. Roll the dough into 1-inch balls. Drop the cookie dough into the bag and shake to cover. With your thumb or the back of a ¼-teaspoon measuring spoon, make an indentation in the center of each cookie. Fill each with ¼ teaspoon jam.

7. Bake one sheet at a time for about 15 minutes, until the cookies are light golden brown on the bottoms. Let cool completely.

Peppermint Meltaways

Makes 24 cookies

Prep time: 10 minutes, plus 2 hours to chill   **Bake time:** 8 to 10 minutes per sheet

These cookies are so soft and buttery they practically melt in your mouth. The peppermint is refreshing and evocative of the holidays, but these cookies are delicious year-round. I love serving them chilled with a bowl of ice cream.

1¼ cups (150g) all-purpose flour

12 tablespoons (1½ sticks, 170g) unsalted butter, at room temperature

½ cup (56g) cornstarch

⅓ cup (38g) powdered sugar

1 teaspoon vanilla extract

½ teaspoon peppermint extract

1. Combine the flour, butter, cornstarch, sugar, vanilla, and peppermint extract in a medium bowl and, using a hand mixer on medium-high speed, mix until thoroughly combined.

2. Place the dough on a sheet of plastic wrap and shape it into a 9-inch-long log. Wrap the log in the plastic and refrigerate for 1 to 2 hours, until firm.

3. Place an oven rack in the center of the oven and preheat to 350°F. Line two rimmed baking sheets with parchment paper.

4. Using a sharp knife, cut the dough log into ¼-inch slices and place on the baking sheets, about 2 inches apart.

5. Bake one sheet at a time for 8 to 10 minutes, until the cookies are set. They will not brown. Let cool completely.

VARIATION TIP: These cookies are delicious on their own, but I also love dipping them in melted white chocolate and sprinkling with crushed candy canes for a pop of color.

Orange-Honey Shortbread

Makes 16 cookies

Prep time: 10 minutes   **Bake time:** 30 to 35 minutes

Shortbread is such a simple cookie to make, but one that yields delicious results. It's also a perfect canvas to use different flavors. In this recipe, I love the sweetness of the honey contrasted with the freshness of the orange.

Nonstick cooking spray

1 cup (2 sticks, 226g) unsalted butter, at room temperature

¼ cup honey

¼ cup (30g) powdered sugar

½ teaspoon vanilla extract

1 tablespoon grated orange zest

2 cups (240g) all-purpose flour

¼ teaspoon salt

1. Place an oven rack in the center of the oven and preheat to 325°F. Grease two 8-inch round cake pans with nonstick spray.

2. In a medium bowl, using a hand mixer on medium-high speed, cream together the butter, honey, and sugar until pale and fluffy, 2 to 3 minutes. Add the vanilla and orange zest and mix well. Add the flour and salt and mix until no flour streaks remain.

3. Divide the dough in half. Press each half into a cake pan. (To keep the dough from sticking to your hands, either dust your hands with flour or mist plastic wrap with cooking spray and use the greased wrap to press the dough into the pans.) Prick the dough all over with a fork for a classic shortbread look.

4. Bake for 30 to 35 minutes, until the cookies are lightly browned.

5. Immediately turn the pans upside down on a cutting board to release the shortbread, then cut each circle of dough into 8 wedges. Transfer the wedges to a cooling rack to cool completely.

VARIATION TIP: After I cool the wedges, I like to dip each triangle into melted dark or white chocolate for an elegant touch.

Seven-Layer Bars

Makes 16 bars

Prep time: 10 minutes   **Bake time:** 25 minutes

You may know these as magic bars or "Hello Dolly" bars. A buttery graham cracker crust is topped with chocolate chips, coconut, and nuts, then sweetened condensed milk is poured over everything. I prefer to add the coconut last so it becomes toasted and crunchy as it bakes. If you prefer a chewier bar, layer the coconut on before adding the condensed milk on top.

Nonstick cooking spray (optional)

8 tablespoons (1 stick, 113g) unsalted butter, melted and slightly cooled

1½ cups (213g) graham cracker crumbs

½ cup (85g) semisweet chocolate chips

½ cup (85g) white chocolate chips

½ cup (85g) butterscotch chips

1 cup (113g) chopped walnuts

1 (14-ounce) can sweetened condensed milk

1¼ cups (107g) sweetened shredded coconut

1. Preheat the oven to 350°F. Line a 9-by-13-inch baking pan with parchment paper, leaving an overhang on the sides to lift the finished bars out, or grease the pan lightly with nonstick cooking spray.

2. In a medium bowl, combine the butter and graham cracker crumbs and stir until combined. Press the crumbs evenly into the bottom of the baking pan.

3. In the following order, sprinkle the semisweet chocolate chips, white chocolate chips, butterscotch chips, and walnuts over the crust. Pour the condensed milk evenly over everything. Top with the coconut.

4. Bake for about 25 minutes, until the top is golden brown. Place the pan on a cooling rack to cool completely, then cut into bars.

SUBSTITUTION TIP: You can use any combination of chocolate chips or nuts, depending on what you have on hand in your pantry, making this a very versatile recipe.

Russian Tea Cakes

Makes 24 cookies

Prep time: 10 minutes, plus 3 hours to chill   **Bake time:** 15 to 20 minutes per sheet

These are also known as Mexican wedding cookies, snowballs, and butterballs. I've also heard of a version with almonds instead of pecans that are called Italian wedding cookies. Whatever you call them, they are melt-in-your-mouth delicious.

1 cup (113g)
 chopped pecans

1 cup (2 sticks, 226g)
 unsalted butter, at room
 temperature

⅔ cup (76g) powdered
 sugar, plus more
 for rolling

1½ teaspoons
 vanilla extract

2 cups (240g)
 all-purpose flour

¼ teaspoon salt

SUBSTITUTION TIP: If you want to make these cookies nut-free, replace the pecans with mini chocolate chips. Obviously, do not toast the chocolate!

1. Preheat the oven to 325°F. Line two rimmed baking sheets with parchment paper.

2. Spread out the pecans on one of the baking sheets. Toast in the oven for 5 minutes, or until slightly browned. Turn off the oven.

3. In a medium bowl, using a hand mixer on medium-high speed, cream together the butter and sugar until pale and fluffy, 2 to 3 minutes. Mix in the vanilla, flour, salt, and toasted pecans. Cover the bowl with plastic wrap and refrigerate for 2 to 3 hours, until firm.

4. Place an oven rack in the center of the oven and preheat to 325°F.

5. Scoop the dough into 1½-inch balls (or form the dough into crescent shapes) and place on the baking sheets, about 2 inches apart.

6. Bake one sheet at a time for 15 to 20 minutes, until the bottoms are light golden brown.

7. While the cookies are baking, put some powdered sugar on a plate or in a shallow bowl. As soon as the cookies come out of the oven, use a spoon to immediately roll the warm cookies in the powdered sugar. Place the cookies on a cooling rack and let cool completely, then roll them in the sugar a second time.

Out-of-This-World Brownies

Makes 12 brownies

Prep time: 20 minutes   **Bake time:** 20 minutes

What's better than a brownie? A brownie with a decadent topping that dances between frosting and glaze. This superthin brownie will remind you of simpler times and lunchbox treats. Enjoy this stroll down memory lane in under an hour.

¼ cup brewed espresso or
  strong coffee
12 tablespoons (1½ sticks,
  169g) unsalted butter,
  at room temperature,
  divided
½ cup (85g) plus ¼ cup
  (43g) chopped semi-
  sweet chocolate, divided
6 tablespoons unsweet-
  ened natural cocoa
  powder, divided
1½ teaspoons salt, divided
1 cup (213g) packed
  brown sugar
1 large egg
1 large egg yolk
1 cup (120g) cake flour
⅓ cup heavy (whip-
  ping) cream
2 cups (227g) powdered
  sugar, divided
1 tablespoon cornstarch
1 tablespoon bourbon or
  vanilla extract
Sprinkles or crushed nuts,
  for topping (optional)

1. Preheat the oven to 350°F. Line a 9-by-13-inch baking pan with parchment paper.

2. In a medium microwave-safe bowl, combine the espresso, 4 tablespoons butter, ½ cup chocolate, 3 tablespoons cocoa, and ½ teaspoon salt. Microwave in 30-second bursts until the butter and chocolate are melted. Whisk to combine.

3. Add the brown sugar, egg, and egg yolk, and whisk to combine. Add the cake flour and whisk. Pour into the pan, using a spatula to spread it evenly (it will be very thin).

4. Bake for 20 minutes, or until the top is matte and the center is firm. Cool completely before frosting.

5. Wash and dry the bowl for the frosting. Combine the remaining 8 tablespoons butter, cream, 3 tablespooons cocoa, and ¼ cup chocolate. Microwave in 30-second bursts until the chocolate and butter are melted. Whisk to combine. Add 1 cup powdered sugar, the cornstarch, and bourbon. Stir until completely incorporated. Add the remaining 1 cup powdered sugar and mix until combined. Pour over the cooled brownies. Top with sprinkles or crushed nuts, if you like.

Linzer Bars

Makes 16 bars

Prep time: 10 minutes   **Bake time:** 20 to 25 minutes

These bars are inspired by the classic Linzer torte that hails from Austria. Typically, they are made into a beautiful sandwich cookie with a peekaboo jam filling. However, that can be quite a daunting task for any baker to undertake. These nutty bars made with sweet raspberry preserves are everything you love about those cookies, but they are ready in just minutes.

Nonstick cooking spray (optional)

1 cup (120g) all-purpose flour

1 cup (96g) almond flour

1 cup (113g) powdered sugar

½ teaspoon ground cinnamon

½ teaspoon salt

8 tablespoons (1 stick, 113g) unsalted butter, at room temperature

1 teaspoon grated lemon zest

1 cup (340g) raspberry jam

1. Place an oven rack in the center of the oven and preheat to 375°F. Line a 9-inch square baking pan with parchment paper or grease lightly with nonstick cooking spray.

2. In a medium bowl, stir together the all-purpose flour, almond flour, powdered sugar, cinnamon, salt, butter, and lemon zest until the mixture is crumbly.

3. Press two-thirds of the dough into the bottom of the pan. Spread the jam on top. Scatter pieces of the remaining dough on top of the jam.

4. Bake for 20 to 25 minutes, until the top is golden. Place the pan on a cooling rack to cool completely, then cover and store in the refrigerator until ready to cut into bars.

SUBSTITUTION TIP: Try mixing things up by using apricot jam instead of raspberry or ground walnuts in place of the almond flour.

Key Lime Coolers

Makes 24 cookies

Prep time: 25 minutes   **Bake time:** 10 minutes

These soft, tender cookies walk the line between cake and cookie. Initially I thought there was nothing spectacular about these cookies, until I looked down and realized I had polished off three of them without even blinking. Consider yourself warned.

8 tablespoons (1 stick, 113g) unsalted butter, at room temperature

1 cup (198g) granulated sugar

1 large egg

1 large egg yolk

2 cups (240g) all-purpose flour

1 teaspoon baking powder

½ teaspoon baking soda

½ teaspoon salt

¼ cup freshly squeezed key lime juice

2 teaspoons grated key lime zest, divided

1 cup (113g) powdered sugar

VARIATION TIP: Instead of topping with powdered sugar, give the cookies a drizzle of melted white chocolate followed by a dusting of lime zest.

1. Preheat the oven to 350°F. Line a rimmed baking sheet with parchment paper.

2. In a medium bowl, using a hand mixer on high speed, combine the butter and sugar until light and fluffy, about 2 minutes. Scrape down the sides of the bowl well. Mix in the egg and egg yolk, scraping down the sides of the bowl as needed. Add the flour, baking powder, baking soda, salt, lime juice, and 1 teaspoon key lime zest. Beat on high speed for 2 minutes, until the mixture is airy and all the ingredients are incorporated.

3. Scoop out 2-tablespoon portions of the dough onto the baking sheet, 2 to 3 inches apart.

4. Bake for 10 minutes, or until golden brown around the edges.

5. While the cookies are baking, wash and dry the bowl. Combine the powdered sugar and remaining 1 teaspoon key lime zest, using a fork to fluff out any clumps.

6. Dust the sugar over the cookies when they come out of the oven. The sugar sticks best while the cookies are still warm. Let cool completely.

SUBSTITUTION TIP: Can't find key limes? It's okay, just use regular limes. It won't be as tart but will still have a lovely flavor.

Potato Chip Cookies

Makes 24 cookies

Prep time: 15 minutes   **Bake time:** 5 to 7 minutes

This recipe was born out of an addiction to caramel sauce. I was looking for something to dip into it. Plain potato chips happened to be in reach, and it was heaven. But what's better than just dipping a chip? Dipping a cookie. There are plenty of potato chip cookies out there, but these are packed with layers of salty, sweet flavor.

1½ cups (35g) plain potato chips, or more as needed

1 cup (2 sticks, 226g) unsalted butter, at room temperature

1 cup (113g) powdered sugar

¼ cup peanut butter

1 teaspoon vanilla extract

1½ cups (180g) all-purpose flour

½ cup (88g) mini chocolate chips

Jarred caramel sauce, for serving

1. Preheat the oven to 350°F. Line a rimmed baking sheet with parchment paper.

2. Put the potato chips in a resealable plastic bag, press out the air, and seal. Smash the chips into smaller pieces. Measure out ¾ cup crushed chips. If the amount is less than ¾ cup, crush additional chips to reach ¾ cup. (If there is more than ¾ cup, snack on any extras.)

3. In a medium bowl, using a hand mixer on medium speed, combine the butter, powdered sugar, peanut butter, and vanilla until fluffy, 2 to 3 minutes. Add the flour and mix until combined. Fold in the potato chips and chocolate chips.

4. Scoop out 2-tablespoon portions of the dough onto the baking sheet.

5. Bake for 5 to 7 minutes, until the edges are golden. Let cool completely.

6. Serve with the caramel sauce, for dipping.

SUBSTITUTION TIP: Instead of peanut butter, you can use another nut butter; to make it completely nut-free, replace the peanut butter with 2 additional tablespoons of butter.

Tasty Tahini Cookies

Makes 24 cookies

Prep time: 20 minutes   **Bake time:** 12 minutes

I'm happiest when I'm playing with new ingredients in my kitchen, so when I was at the grocery store and happened upon a container of tahini, a paste made of ground sesame seeds, I threw it in my basket and started scheming. Tahini has a lovely nutty scent and a texture similar to that of natural peanut butter, making it a great alternative for someone with a nut allergy. These cookies have a lightly sweet flavor with a nutty quality, but they don't give you that punch-in-the-mouth thickness that peanut butter cookies can have.

8 tablespoons (1 stick, 113g) unsalted butter, at room temperature

1 packed cup (213g) light brown sugar

½ cup (99g) granulated sugar

⅓ cup tahini

1 large egg

1 large egg yolk

2 cups (240g) all-purpose flour

½ teaspoon salt

½ teaspoon baking soda

1 teaspoon vanilla extract

¼ cup black sesame seeds

1. Preheat the oven to 350°F. Line a rimmed baking sheet with parchment paper.

2. In a medium bowl, using a hand mixer on medium speed, cream the butter, brown sugar, granulated sugar, and tahini until fluffy, about 2 minutes. Mix in the egg and egg yolk, scraping down the sides of the bowl if necessary. Add the flour, salt, baking soda, and vanilla and mix until combined.

3. Put the sesame seeds on a plate or in a shallow bowl. Scoop out 2-tablespoon portions of the dough and roll them into balls. Roll the balls in the sesame seeds to coat, then place on the baking sheet.

4. Bake for 12 minutes, or until the edges are golden and the cookies do not look shiny. The finished cookies will be soft throughout. Let cool completely. (If you don't want to bake all 24 cookies at once, just scoop the dough, roll the balls in the sesame seeds, and freeze them. Pull a few out whenever you need a quick snack and bake from frozen.)

VARIATION TIP: Instead of black sesame seeds, roll the cookies in sanding sugar to give them a crunchy texture.

Hazelnut Sandy Sandwich Cookies

Makes 6 dozen sandwich cookies

Prep time: 45 minutes   **Bake time:** 30 minutes

This recipe makes a ton of tiny cookies! I mean, who wouldn't want to eat a handful of tiny cookies? Since this recipe makes so many tiny cookies, I pipe out the dough with a piping bag and a large round tip, but feel free to use a gallon-size freezer bag with a corner snipped off.

1 heaping cup (89g) hazelnuts

12 tablespoons (1½ sticks, 169g) unsalted butter, at room temperature

1 cup (113g) powdered sugar

1¼ cups (150g) all-purpose flour

2 tablespoons unsweetened natural cocoa powder

½ teaspoon salt

½ cup chocolate-hazelnut spread

1. Preheat the oven to 350°F. Line two rimmed baking sheets with parchment paper.

2. Place the hazelnuts on one of the baking sheets and bake for 10 minutes. Wrap the warm hazelnuts in a clean kitchen towel and rub off as much skin as you can. Reduce the oven temperature to 300°F. Let the sheet pan cool completely.

3. Transfer the hazelnuts to a food processor and pulse until there are no visible lumps. Add the butter, powdered sugar, flour, cocoa, and salt and pulse to combine. The dough will be very wet and slightly chunky.

4. Transfer the dough to a piping bag fitted with a 2D or comparable round piping tip. Pipe the dough into 1-inch disks onto the baking sheets; they can be close together. Each baking sheet should fit around 70 cookies.

5. Bake for 30 minutes, or until the cookies are firm and dry. Let cool completely.

6. Once cooled, put the hazelnut spread in a piping bag (no tip needed, just a small hole). Squeeze a small amount onto one cookie and sandwich with a second cookie.

Peanut and Pretzel Florentines

Makes 12 sandwich cookies

Prep time: 20 minutes, plus cooling **Bake time:** 10 minutes

Florentines are impossibly fancy-seeming cookies typically made with sliced almonds. I turn them on their head by swapping in pretzels and peanuts for the almonds. They're shatteringly crisp and delicious and relatively quick to make.

¼ cup (49g) granu-
   lated sugar

3 tablespoons heavy
   (whipping) cream

2 tablespoons honey

1 tablespoon
   unsalted butter

1 cup (40g) pretzels (I use
   mini twists)

⅓ cup (35g) salted peanuts

¼ cup creamy
   peanut butter

1. Preheat the oven to 350°F. Line two rimmed baking sheets with parchment paper.

2. In a small saucepan over medium-high heat, stir together the sugar, cream, honey, and butter. Bring to a boil for 30 seconds, stirring constantly. Remove the pan from the heat.

3. Put the pretzels in a resealable bag, press out the air, and seal. Smash the pretzels into ¼-inch or so pieces with a rolling pin. Roughly smash or chop the peanuts with a rolling pin or knife (or use a food processor). You should have about ½ cup pretzel pieces and ¼ cup crushed peanuts.

4. Add the peanuts and pretzels to the syrup mixture and carefully stir to combine. Allow to cool for 5 minutes.

5. Scoop 2-teaspoon mounds onto the baking sheets, 3 to 5 inches apart, keeping the pretzels and peanuts in a single layer as much as possible. The syrup will spread quite a bit, and if the peanuts and pretzels are concentrated in the center, it's going to make an unbalanced cookie.

6. Bake for 10 minutes, until the cookies have spread and become thin and golden brown. Watch them carefully, because they burn quickly.

7. Cool the cookies on the pan; they will set up as they cool. Once cool, carefully remove them with a spatula. Take care; the cookies are delicate.

8. Carefully spread a thin layer of peanut butter on the back of one cookie and sandwich with the back of another. The cookies will keep in an airtight container at room temperature for up to 5 days.

SUBSTITUTION TIP: If you have a peanut allergy, replace the peanuts with the same amount of pretzels and use melted chocolate for sandwiching them.

Chocolate Sandwich Cookies

Makes 24 sandwich cookies

Prep time: 45 minutes   **Bake time:** 9 minutes

Obviously I think sugar and butter are delightful, but I do try to eat them in moderation—except when it comes to these cookies. I can inhale them all day if nobody is around to watch. These have the same rich chocolate flavor I remember from my childhood, thanks to the Dutch-process cocoa, but in a soft baked version.

For the cookies

- 1 cup (2 sticks, 226g) unsalted butter, at room temperature
- 1 cup (198g) granulated sugar
- ⅔ cup (56g) unsweetened natural cocoa powder
- ⅓ cup (28g) Dutch-process cocoa powder
- 2 large eggs
- 2½ cups (300g) cake flour, plus more to press the cookies
- ¼ teaspoon baking powder
- ¼ teaspoon salt

1. Preheat the oven to 375°F. Line a rimmed baking sheet with parchment paper.

2. In a medium bowl, using a hand mixer on medium speed, combine the butter and granulated sugar until fluffy, 2 to 3 minutes. Scrape down the sides of the bowl and add the natural cocoa and Dutch-process cocoa. On low speed, blend until combined. Add the eggs, increase the speed to medium, and mix to combine, scraping down the sides of the bowl as needed. Add the flour, baking powder, and salt. Mix to combine.

3. Scoop out 1-tablespoon portions of the dough and roll them into balls. Place the balls on the baking sheet. They won't spread too much, so they can be close together. Dip the bottom of a glass in flour and gently press down on each dough ball to create a thin cookie. They should be about 2 inches wide and ¼ inch thick.

4. Bake for 9 minutes, or until the tops of the cookies no longer look glossy. Let cool completely.

For the buttercream

8 tablespoons (1 stick, 113g) unsalted butter, at room temperature

½ cup vegetable shortening

½ teaspoon vanilla extract

½ teaspoon almond extract

1 teaspoon salt

4 cups (454g) powdered sugar

1 to 2 tablespoons water (optional)

5. While the cookies bake, wash and dry the bowl to make the buttercream. Using a hand mixer on low speed, whip the butter, shortening, vanilla, almond extract, and salt until incorporated. Scrape down the sides of the bowl, then increase the speed to medium-high for 3 minutes, until the mixture is light and fluffy. It should almost double in volume.

6. Reduce the mixer's speed to low. Add the powdered sugar in two additions, mixing fully between additions and scraping down the sides of the bowl as needed. If needed, add water, 1 tablespoon at a time, to achieve a spreadable consistency. The buttercream should be smooth, light, and fluffy.

7. Spoon a small amount of buttercream on the bottom of one cooled cookie, then top with a second cookie to make a sandwich.

VARIATION TIP: Want to have some fun? Color the frosting to match the theme of your party, or roll the exposed edges of the frosting in sprinkles or nonpareils for extra color and texture.

Matcha Cookies

Makes 16 cookies

Prep time: 10 minutes   **Bake time:** 12 minutes

Matcha is made from the ground leaves of young tea bushes. There are some indi-cations that it has some healing properties, everything from improving your skin to helping fight cancer. I am a pastry chef, not a doctor, but I do know that these cookies are tasty and tea is calming, so in my book that makes them a health food.

½ **cup solid coconut oil**

⅔ **cup (132g)**
   granulated sugar

1 large egg

1 teaspoon vanilla extract

1⅔ **cups (200g)**
   all-purpose flour

2 teaspoons
   matcha powder

½ **teaspoon salt**

½ **teaspoon baking powder**

¼ **cup demerara sugar,**
   for coating

1. Preheat the oven to 350°F. Line a rimmed baking sheet with parchment paper.

2. In a medium bowl, using a hand mixer on medium speed, beat the coconut oil and sugar until light and fluffy, 2 to 3 minutes. Add the egg and vanilla and beat to incorporate, scraping down the sides of the bowl as needed.

3. Mix in the flour, matcha, salt, and baking powder. Beat on high for 1 minute, as these cookies need a bit of air in them.

4. Put the demerara sugar in a small resealable bag. Scoop out 2-tablespoon portions of the dough and carefully roll them into balls. One at a time, add the dough balls to the bag and gently shake it to coat in sugar. Place each cookie on the baking sheet, 2 to 3 inches apart.

5. Bake for 12 minutes, or until the edges are golden and the cookies have puffed up slightly. Let cool completely.

INGREDIENT TIP: You can find matcha powder in the tea and coffee section of your grocery store. Look for one that is labeled "culinary grade."

Chocolate Chip and Cashew Skillet Cookie

Serves 8

Prep time: 20 minutes   **Bake time:** 25 minutes

This dessert is fun to serve for a group (who doesn't love eating warm cookies straight from the pan?) and you can switch out the mix-ins for a variety of delicious cookie options. The brown butter is an extra step, but it's worth it for the flavor—and I make up for it in effort by going from stovetop to oven with no extra dishes.

8 tablespoons (1 stick, 113g) unsalted butter

⅓ packed cup (71g) brown sugar

⅓ cup (66g) granulated sugar

2 large eggs

1⅓ cups (160g) all-purpose flour

1 teaspoon salt

1 teaspoon baking soda

½ teaspoon baking powder

1 cup (170g) chocolate chips

½ cup (56g) chopped cashews

½ cup cashew butter

1. Preheat the oven to 350°F.

2. In a 9- or 10-inch skillet, melt the butter over medium-high heat until it begins to take on a golden-brown color and a nutty aroma, about 5 minutes. Watch it carefully, as you don't want to let it burn.

3. Remove the skillet from the heat, add the brown sugar and granulated sugar, and whisk until combined. Allow to cool for 5 minutes, then add the eggs, flour, salt, baking soda, and baking powder. Carefully fold in the chocolate chips and cashews.

4. Drop in scoops of cashew butter and swirl them into the batter with a spoon. Don't overmix, as you want big, visible swirls.

5. Place the skillet in the oven and bake for 25 minutes for a gooey cookie with some give in the center. The top will be golden brown when done. If you want a firmer, sliceable cookie, continue baking for another 5 minutes.

SUBSTITUTION TIP: While I adore the addition of the cashews and cashew butter, you can switch them out for any nut and nut butter or you can leave them out entirely.

Chapter 3
Quick Breads, Muffins, and Scones

These recipes are easy enough to be a weekday treat, but flavorful and fun enough to still make any brunch or breakfast feel festive, even if it's just another Sunday.

Pancetta and Rosemary Scones
page 44

Almond-Apricot Scones

Makes 8 scones

Prep time: 15 minutes, plus 15 minutes to chill   **Bake time:** 17 minutes

Instead of cutting in butter and carefully working the dough, I use room-temperature butter and put the scones in the refrigerator to firm back up so they'll keep their shape in the oven. The scones are still delicious without this chill time; they just look like giant cookies. The almond comes in three forms, each adding a different element: almond extract for deep flavor, almond flour for tenderness, and slivered almonds for crunch.

1⅓ cups (160g)
   all-purpose flour
½ cup (48g) almond flour
⅓ cup (66g) granu-
   lated sugar
1 teaspoon baking powder
¼ teaspoon baking soda
¼ teaspoon salt
6 tablespoons (¾ stick,
   85g) unsalted butter, at
   room temperature
½ cup heavy (whipping)
   cream, plus more for
   brushing
¼ cup (32g) diced dried
   apricots
¼ cup (29g) slivered
   almonds, plus more for
   sprinkling

1. Preheat the oven to 400°F. Line a rimmed baking sheet with parchment paper.

2. In a medium bowl, combine the flour, almond flour, sugar, baking powder, baking soda, and salt. Use a fork to whisk everything together.

3. Add the butter to the flour mixture using the fork until evenly distributed and well broken up.

4. Add the heavy cream and combine with the fork. The dough will be crumbly and might look like it won't come together, but it will. You might need to switch to your hands at the end to pull in some of the crumbs in the bottom of the bowl, being careful not to overwork the dough. Add the apricots and slivered almonds and mix until just incorporated.

5. Using a ¼-cup scoop, place eight equal mounds of dough on the baking sheet. Do not press down. Brush the tops with heavy cream and sprinkle with slivered almonds.

6. Place the pan in the refrigerator for 15 minutes, or until well chilled.

7. Bake for 17 minutes, or until the edges of the scones are brown and the tops are glossy. The scones will spring back when lightly pressed.

SUBSTITUTION TIP: If you don't have dried apricots, try raisins, cranberries, or even mini chocolate chips.

Strawberry Weekday Biscuits

Makes 6 biscuits

Prep time: 20 minutes **Bake time:** 17 to 20 minutes

Growing up, our big "weekend breakfast" always included a can of biscuits. I eagerly slathered mine with strawberry jam and butter. I never understood why we only had biscuits on the weekend. Why not more weekday biscuits? Should sticky smiles be relegated to the already happy weekend? I think not. Make these biscuits the night before and pop them into the oven for a quick weekday morning smile.

3 cups (360g) all-purpose flour

¼ cup (49g) granulated sugar

1½ teaspoons baking powder

1 teaspoon baking soda

½ teaspoon salt

¼ cup vegetable shortening

4 tablespoons (½ stick, 56g) unsalted butter, at room temperature

1 teaspoon active dry yeast

1 tablespoon warm water

½ cup (15g) crumbled freeze-dried strawberries

½ cup buttermilk, plus more for brushing

Strawberry jam, for serving (optional)

1. (If you plan to bake the biscuits the next morning, skip to step 2.) Preheat the oven to 400°F. Line a rimmed baking sheet with parchment paper.

2. In a medium bowl, combine the flour, sugar, baking powder, baking soda, and salt. Combine the ingredients with a fork.

3. Cut the shortening and butter into the dry ingredients using a fork or pastry cutter. Once fully combined, it should be dry and crumbly with small, pea-size bits throughout.

4. Make a small well in the center of the mixture and add the yeast. Top it with the warm water. Stir slightly to combine the water and yeast. Allow this to sit for about 5 minutes, until the yeast begins to bloom and bubble.

5. After 5 minutes, use the fork to stir the yeast into the flour mixture. Sprinkle the crumbled strawberries over the mixture and stir to combine.

6. Pour half of the buttermilk over the top and stir to combine. Pour in the remaining buttermilk and stir until just combined.

7. Using your hands, begin kneading the dough in the bowl, until it is a single combined disk and no dry pieces remain. Be careful not to overwork the dough; knead just until it comes together.

8. Place the dough on the baking sheet. Using your palm, press the dough into a rectangle roughly 6 inches long, 4 inches wide, and ½ inch thick. Cut the rectangle into six 2-inch-square biscuits. Space out the biscuits slightly on the baking sheet.

9. Brush the tops of the biscuits with a bit more buttermilk. (If baking the next morning, cover with plastic wrap and refrigerate overnight. In the morning, preheat the oven to 400°F.)

10. Bake for 17 to 20 minutes, until the tops are golden brown and the biscuits have risen to about 1 inch tall.

11. Split the biscuits and fill with strawberry jam, if using.

Pancetta and Rosemary Scones

Makes 8 scones

Prep time: 20 minutes   **Bake time:** 25 minutes

I've always leaned toward sweet scones with thick glaze oozing over the top. But there's something soothing about the smell of fresh rosemary lightly baked in the pan drippings of pancetta that makes these savory scones downright irresistible. I keep a jar of equal parts honey and butter in my refrigerator at all times. I brush it on these scones after they come out of the oven, and it's also great drizzled on fried chicken (it will change your life).

½ cup (57g) diced
   pancetta
1 heaping tablespoon
   chopped fresh rosemary
2½ cups (300g)
   all-purpose flour
1 tablespoon granulated
   sugar
1 teaspoon salt
1 tablespoon
   baking powder
¼ teaspoon garlic powder
8 tablespoons (1 stick,
   113g) plus 1 tablespoon
   cold unsalted
   butter, divided
½ cup grated cheddar
   cheese
1 cup heavy (whipping)
   cream, plus more for
   brushing
1 tablespoon honey
Freshly cracked black
   pepper, for sprinkling

1. Preheat the oven to 425°F. Line a rimmed baking sheet with parchment paper.

2. Spread out the pancetta on the baking sheet and bake for 5 minutes, stirring occasionally, until the fat is rendering out and the pancetta begins to brown. After 5 minutes, stir in the rosemary to release its oils and bake for another 5 minutes, until the pancetta is browned. Set aside to cool.

3. In a medium microwave-safe bowl, stir together the flour, sugar, salt, baking powder, and garlic powder. Using the large holes on a box grater, grate 8 tablespoons butter into the flour mixture, pausing to toss the flour over the butter occasionally. Once grated, use your fingers to break up any butter clumps and distribute the mixture evenly. Add the pancetta and rosemary mixture and the cheddar cheese. Toss to combine.

4. Slowly add the cream, pausing to fluff the mixture with one hand as you go. Once all the cream has been added, use the heel of your palm to push the dough down into the bottom and side of the bowl, then grab an edge and fold it over the rest of the dough. Spin the bowl and repeat, kneading the dough and incorporating the bits in the bottom of the bowl.

5. Once combined, place the dough on the baking sheet and pat it into a circle about 8 inches across and 1 inch thick. Cut the circle into 8 wedges and space them out on the pan. Brush the tops of the scones with some cream.

6. Bake for 15 minutes, or until the scones have risen and are golden brown.

7. While the scones are baking, wash and dry the bowl. Put the remaining 1 tablespoon butter and the honey in the bowl and microwave until melted, about 30 seconds.

8. When the scones come out of the oven, brush the tops with the honey-butter mixture and sprinkle with cracked pepper. Serve warm or at room temperature.

SUBSTITUTION TIP: Don't have fresh rosemary? Dried will work in a pinch; just use 2 teaspoons.

Honey-Walnut Muffins

Makes 12 muffins

Prep time: 10 minutes   **Bake time:** 25 minutes

My husband has been asking me to bake things with less sugar and fewer carbs, and it's the saddest thing ever, if you ask me. But I aim to please, so I came up with these tasty muffins: crunchy walnuts add flavor and texture, while almond flour and oats keep it gluten-free without having to break out the more complicated ingredients. Be sure to seek out oats labeled "gluten-free" on the package; if they're not certified gluten-free, they might be cross-contaminated. The yogurt and honey round out the flavors while staying a touch healthier.

½ cup milk

½ cup (90g) old-fashioned rolled oats

4 tablespoons (½ stick, 56g) unsalted butter, at room temperature

¼ cup (49g) granulated sugar

¼ cup (84g) honey

½ cup honey-flavored yogurt

1 large egg

2 cups (192g) almond flour

1 teaspoon baking powder

½ teaspoon baking soda

½ teaspoon salt

½ cup (57g) chopped walnuts

1. Preheat the oven to 375°F. Line a 12-cup muffin tin with paper liners.

2. In a medium bowl, combine the milk and oats and let stand for 5 minutes to allow the oats to soften.

3. After 5 minutes, add the butter, sugar, honey, and yogurt and mix to combine. Add the egg and mix again.

4. Add the almond flour, baking powder, baking soda, and salt and stir to combine. Fold in the walnuts.

5. Using a scoop or two spoons, evenly distribute the batter between the lined muffin cups, making sure not to fill each cup more than three-fourths full.

6. Bake for 25 minutes, or until the tops are golden. Serve warm or at room temperature.

INGREDIENT TIP: Yogurt comes in so many different flavors, and it's an easy way to add layers of flavor to baked goods. While I use honey-flavored yogurt here, a plain or other flavored yogurt would work equally well.

Cinnamon-Raisin Bread

Makes 1 loaf

Prep time: 10 minutes **Bake time:** 55 minutes

When I used to think of cinnamon-raisin bread, a yeasted, swirled bread came to mind. This soft, sweet, aromatic quick bread studded with plump, chewy raisins delivers on the flavor in much less time. It makes for a lovely breakfast or afternoon snack. Don't skimp on the crunchy sugar on top.

Nonstick cooking spray

5⅓ tablespoons (⅓ cup, 75g) unsalted butter, at room temperature

1 packed cup (213g) light brown sugar

2 large eggs

2 cups (240g) all-purpose flour

1 teaspoon baking powder

1 teaspoon baking soda

1 teaspoon ground cinnamon

½ teaspoon salt

1 cup sour cream

1 cup golden raisins

3 tablespoons demerara sugar

1. Preheat the oven to 350°F. Grease a 10-inch loaf pan with nonstick cooking spray or make a parchment-paper sling (see Technique tip).

2. In a medium bowl, using a hand mixer, cream the butter and brown sugar until light and fluffy. Add the eggs and mix until well incorporated.

3. Add the flour, baking powder, baking soda, cinnamon, salt, and sour cream and mix until well incorporated. Fold in the raisins.

4. Pour the batter into the loaf pan and smooth out the top. Sprinkle the demerara sugar over the top.

5. Bake for 55 minutes, or until a toothpick inserted into the center comes out clean. Let the bread cool for 10 to 15 minutes, then remove the bread from the pan.

INGREDIENT TIP: I use golden raisins, which might look a bit different than the classic cinnamon-raisin bread. I like that they're sweeter and plumper, so it's worth the change in aesthetics.

TECHNIQUE TIP: A parchment-paper sling is an easy way to line a pan without any tricky folding or measuring. Cut a piece of parchment paper the length of the loaf pan, long enough so it covers the bottom of the pan, up both sides of the pan, and hangs over the edges. Use cooking spray to hold it in place. Then just lift out the bread easily once it has cooled.

Peanut Butter–Banana Muffins

Makes 12 muffins

Prep time: 10 minutes   **Bake time:** 20 minutes

These muffins are moist and have the best crumb. They should be called "banana–peanut butter muffins," because they have more banana flavor than peanut butter flavor, but that doesn't roll off the tongue as well. These muffins are not overly sweet (as some muffins can be), so you can eat one or four.

8 tablespoons (1 stick, 113g) unsalted butter

¼ cup creamy or chunky peanut butter

2 ripe bananas

½ packed cup (106g) brown sugar

2 large eggs

2 cups (240g) all-purpose flour

2 teaspoons baking powder

½ teaspoon baking soda

½ teaspoon salt

¼ cup milk

1. Preheat the oven to 350°F. Line a 12-cup muffin tin with paper liners.

2. In a medium microwave-safe bowl, combine the butter and peanut butter. Microwave until melted, about 30 seconds, then whisk to combine.

3. Add the bananas and use a fork to mash them into small bits. Add the brown sugar and whisk to combine.

4. Add the eggs one at a time, whisking to combine between additions. Add the flour, baking powder, baking soda, and salt. Continue whisking, making sure to get out any flour lumps.

5. Add the milk and whisk to combine.

6. Divide the batter evenly among the muffin cups.

7. Bake for 20 minutes, or until the muffins are golden and the tops spring back at your touch.

VARIATION TIP: To take these muffins from breakfast to dessert, fold ½ cup of chocolate chips into the batter before filling the muffin cups.

Sweet Potato Bread

Makes 1 loaf

Prep time: 15 minutes   **Bake time:** 1 hour

If you love pumpkin, then you will absolutely freak out over this Sweet Potato Bread. It's got the same aromatic warmth as pumpkin bread, but with the added benefit of being completely vegan. It's dense but sweet, like the filling of a sweet potato pie. Serve warm for a dessert-like treat.

1 medium sweet potato

1 packed cup (213g)
  brown sugar

2 teaspoons
  baking powder

½ teaspoon baking soda

½ teaspoon salt

½ teaspoon ground
  cinnamon

¼ teaspoon ground
  cardamom

¼ teaspoon
  ground nutmeg

½ cup applesauce

½ cup vegetable oil

1 cup (120g)
  all-purpose flour

1 cup (120g) cake flour

½ cup almond milk or milk
  of your choice

¼ cup pepitas (optional)

1. Preheat the oven to 375°F. Line an 8-inch loaf pan with a parchment-paper sling (see Technique tip on page 47).

2. Prick the sweet potato all over with a fork and place it on a microwave-safe plate. Microwave until the sweet potato is soft—start with 5 minutes, then continue to cook as needed in 1-minute increments. Let cool slightly, then slice open and mash the flesh with a fork. Measure out 1 cup mashed sweet potato.

3. Meanwhile, in a medium bowl, combine the brown sugar, baking powder, baking soda, salt, cinnamon, cardamom, and nutmeg. Add the applesauce and oil and mix to combine.

4. Add the mashed sweet potato and use a fork to combine the mixture.

5. Add the all-purpose flour and cake flour and mix to combine. Add the almond milk and mix until there are no lumps. Pour the batter into the loaf pan. Sprinkle the pepitas on top of the loaf, if using.

6. Bake for 30 minutes, then reduce the oven temperature to 350°F and bake for 30 minutes more, or until the top is golden, the center feels firm, and a toothpick inserted into the bread comes out dry.

Big Ol' Biscuits

Makes 6 biscuits

Prep time: 20 minutes, plus 15 minutes to chill   **Bake time:** 20 minutes

To me, there are very few things in life more Southern than a big ol' biscuit. I prefer mine slathered with butter and honey or some preserves. Of course, these are substantial enough to hold some bacon, egg, and cheese. The lard is a classic Southern ingredient and adds unmatched flavor and moisture. I also use cake flour to give the biscuits a light crumb and help balance their heft.

2¼ cups (270g) all-purpose flour, plus extra for dusting

1¼ cups (156g) cake flour

1 tablespoon sugar

1 tablespoon baking powder

1½ teaspoons baking soda

1 teaspoon salt

¼ cup lard or vegetable shortening

12 tablespoons (1½ sticks, 170g) cold unsalted butter, divided

1 cup buttermilk

3 tablespoons honey

Maldon sea salt, for topping

1. In a medium bowl, combine the all-purpose flour, cake flour, sugar, baking powder, baking soda, and salt. Add the lard and use your fingers to crumble it into the flour mixture, tossing frequently to distribute the fat among the flour.

2. Using the large holes of a box grater, grate 8 tablespoons (1 stick) butter into the mixture, pausing to toss the shredded butter with the flour mixture (the goal is to avoid clumps of butter).

3. Pour in the buttermilk in three additions, using your hand to mix between pours. I make a claw with my right hand and fold the flour into the buttermilk. Once all the buttermilk is incorporated, use the heel of your palm to gently press the dough into the side of the bowl. Turn and repeat all the way around the bowl.

4. Dust a rimmed baking sheet with some all-purpose flour. Scrape the dough onto the pan. Using your hands, form a rectangle about 9 inches long, 6 inches wide, and ½ inch thick. Cut the rectangle in half lengthwise, then in thirds crosswise to make 6 square biscuits.

5. Chill the dough in the refrigerator for at least 15 minutes. While the biscuits chill, preheat the oven to 425°F.

6. Bake the biscuits for 20 minutes, or until the tops are golden. Gently open a biscuit with a knife and look at the center: It should appear crumbly and moist, but not wet.

7. While the biscuits are baking, in a small microwave-safe bowl, combine the remaining 4 tablespoons (½ stick) butter and the honey. Melt in the microwave, and stir to combine. Brush this mixture over the tops of the finished biscuits. Sprinkle with the Maldon sea salt.

SUBSTITUTION TIP: If you don't have cake flour, it's okay to use all-purpose flour. The crumb won't be as fine, but it'll still delicious.

Zucchini-Apple Bread

Makes 1 loaf

Prep time: 20 minutes   **Bake time:** 55 minutes

I remember making muffins and other quick breads as a kid. They're super simple, and you just need a bowl and a spoon. Zucchini bread is such a fun and easy way to sneak something healthy into a baked good. Apple bumps up the sweetness naturally, so I reduce the sugar a little in the recipe.

Nonstick cooking spray
1 medium zucchini
1 apple, peeled and cored
¾ cup (148g) granu-
   lated sugar
½ packed cup (106g) light
   brown sugar
¾ cup vegetable oil
2 large eggs
2¼ cups (270g)
   all-purpose flour
½ teaspoon baking powder
½ teaspoon baking soda
½ teaspoon salt
½ cup chopped pecans or
   walnuts (optional)

1. Preheat the oven to 350°F. Spray a 9-by-5-inch loaf pan with cooking spray.

2. Using the coarsest holes on a box grater, grate the zucchini and the apple. Measure out a total of 2 cups grated apple-zucchini mixture. Set aside.

3. In a medium bowl, combine the granulated sugar, brown sugar, oil, eggs, flour, baking powder, baking soda, and salt. Mix to combine. Fold in the grated zucchini and apple and the nuts (if using). Pour the mixture into the loaf pan.

4. Bake for 55 minutes. After about 45 minutes, if the top is getting too dark, move the pan to the bottom oven rack or tent a piece of aluminum foil over the bread to prevent burning. When done, the bread will spring back lightly when pressed, the top will no longer appear wet, and a tooth-pick inserted into the bread will come out clean. Remove from the oven and cool completely before removing the bread from the pan.

VARIATION TIP: Before baking, sprinkle demerara sugar or chopped nuts over the top for added crunch.

Five-Spice Pear Muffins

Makes 12 muffins

Prep time: 20 minutes   **Bake time:** 15 minutes

These muffins will feel familiar, but they have an unusual pairing of Chinese five-spice powder and pears. Chinese five-spice powder is a combination of cinnamon, cloves, fennel, star anise, and Szechuan pepper. It has a sweet yet spicy flavor, perfect for when you're craving something different. I like to cook my fruit down just a bit to soften it before baking, which is also an opportunity to infuse a bit more flavor.

1 pear, cored, peeled, and diced (use your favorite—I like Bartlett)

6 tablespoons (¾ stick, 85g) unsalted butter, at room temperature, divided

½ packed cup (106g) plus 2 packed tablespoons light brown sugar

½ teaspoon ground cinnamon

¼ cup chopped walnuts

½ cup sour cream

1 large egg

1¼ cups (156g) all-purpose flour

½ teaspoon baking powder

½ teaspoon baking soda

½ teaspoon salt

½ teaspoon Chinese five-spice powder

1. Preheat the oven to 400°F. Line a 12-cup muffin tin with paper liners.

2. in a medium saucepan over medium heat, combine the pear, 2 tablespoons butter, 2 tablespoons brown sugar, cinnamon, and walnuts. Cook for 3 minutes, or until the pears are slightly soft and the fruit and walnuts begin to caramelize. Remove the pan from the heat and allow to cool slightly.

3. Stir in the remaining 4 tablespoons butter, the sour cream, and the remaining ½ cup brown sugar. The butter might melt from the residual heat, which is okay. Add the egg, flour, baking powder, baking soda, salt, and Chinese five-spice powder and stir to combine.

4. Scoop ¼ cup of batter into each muffin cup.

5. Bake for 15 minutes, or until the tops are golden brown.

SUBSTITUTION TIP: Don't have a pear on hand? Just substitute an apple. It has a similar texture and flavor.

Candied Jalapeño Bacon Corn Bread

Serves 12

Prep time: 45 minutes   **Bake time:** 20 minutes

Yes, my corn bread has sugar in it, but I promise it's not "sweet." In the same way that salt balances sweetness in desserts, the sugar here balances the spice and overall flavor of corn bread. This corn bread is the perfect accompaniment to a bowl of chili or a plate piled with Southern favorites. The majority of the prep time is spent making the bacon. The rest of the batter comes together quickly and easily.

For the candied bacon

6 bacon slices, chopped

½ cup pickled jalapeño slices

¼ packed cup (53g) brown sugar

1 teaspoon cayenne pepper

1. Preheat the oven to 425°F.

2. To make the candied bacon, line a 10-inch cast-iron skillet with aluminum foil. (If you don't have a skillet, an 8-inch baking pan will work.) Scatter the bacon and jalapeños in the skillet. Sprinkle the brown sugar and cayenne over the top.

3. Bake until the bacon becomes sticky and crispy, about 15 minutes. Remove from the oven and transfer to a cutting board as soon as it's cool enough to touch. (If you wait too long, the sugar will harden and the bacon will stick to the foil.) Roughly chop the candied bacon and jalapeños. Set aside 1 cup for the recipe and reserve the rest for another use (like snacking). Discard the foil in the skillet.

4. Return the skillet to the hot oven. This will give the corn bread a crunchy exterior once baked.

For the corn bread

8 tablespoons (1 stick, 113g) unsalted butter

1 cup (120g) all-purpose flour

1 cup (150g) cornmeal

2 tablespoons granulated sugar

1½ teaspoons baking powder

1½ teaspoons baking soda

½ teaspoon salt

1½ cups buttermilk

2 large eggs

5. In a medium microwave-safe bowl, melt the butter in the microwave. Add the flour, cornmeal, granulated sugar, baking powder, baking soda, and salt and stir to combine. Pour in the buttermilk and whisk to combine. Add the eggs last, so the warm butter doesn't scramble the eggs.

6. Fold the candied bacon and jalapeños into the batter. Remove the skillet from the oven and carefully pour the batter into it.

7. Bake for 20 minutes, or until the top of the corn bread is golden and the edges are crisp.

Chapter 4
Cakes and Cupcakes

I love cake. It's such a versatile dessert—it can be a sheet cake, a Bundt, a loaf, or cupcakes; you can stack it, roll it, and even set it on fire (baked Alaska, anyone?). You can frost a cake, glaze it, add crunchy sugar to it, or leave it plain (my personal favorite). Serve cake warm, at room temperature, or chilled. Whether you're celebrating a big event or it's just a Tuesday, cake is always the answer. I use a variety of techniques in this chapter, but the result is all the same: yummy, yummy cake.

Pistachio Layer Cake with Cherry Frosting
page 70

Chocolate Cupcakes for Everyone

Makes 12 cupcakes

Prep time: 25 minutes   **Bake time:** 25 minutes

I originally made these cupcakes for a friend's birthday—she happens to be vegan, so she doesn't always get to partake in goodies. Best of all? These vegan cupcakes will work for all your party people. Plus, this is a pantry bake—no unusual ingredients required—and it comes together with a whisk and a bowl—so no unusual tools are required, either. The frosting recipe makes enough to top a dozen cupcakes or frost a sheet cake. A double recipe will fill and decorate a standard 8-inch round layer cake.

For the cupcakes

**1½ cups (180g)
  all-purpose flour**
**1 cup (198g) granulated
  sugar**
**⅓ cup (28g) unsweetened
  natural cocoa powder**
1 teaspoon baking soda
½ teaspoon salt
**⅔ cup almond milk or milk
  of your choice**
**⅓ cup strongly brewed
  coffee or espresso**
¼ cup vegetable oil
1 teaspoon vanilla extract

1. Preheat the oven to 325°F. Line a 12-cup muffin tin with paper liners.

2. In a medium bowl, combine the flour, sugar, cocoa powder, baking soda, and salt and whisk to combine. Add the almond milk, coffee, oil, and vanilla and whisk until all lumps are gone.

3. Scoop the batter into each muffin cup, making sure not to fill them more than three-fourths full.

4. Bake for 25 minutes, or until the center springs back when lightly touched.

5. Let cool for 10 minutes in the pan, then remove the cupcakes and cool completely.

For the frosting

½ cup coconut oil
⅓ cup boiling water
½ cup (42g) unsweetened natural cocoa powder
1 teaspoon vanilla extract
½ teaspoon salt
4 cups (454g) powdered sugar, plus more if needed
2 to 3 tablespoons water (optional)
Sprinkles, for topping

6. While the cupcakes are baking and cooling, wash and dry the bowl for the frosting. Combine the coconut oil, boiling water, and cocoa powder and mix until the coconut oil is melted and the mixture is combined. It might look a bit clumpy, but it will smooth out. Add the vanilla, salt, and 2 cups powdered sugar and mix until combined. Scrape the sides and bottom of the bowl, add the remaining 2 cups powdered sugar, and mix until the frosting is smooth and holds a peak. If the mixture is too dry, add water, 1 tablespoon at a time, until the frosting is smooth. If it's too wet and won't hold a peak, add a few tablespoons more powdered sugar until the frosting thickens.

7. Once the cupcakes are completely cool, use a 2-tablespoon measuring spoon to drop a scoop of frosting on top of each cupcake and swirl it with a spatula. (Alternatively, transfer the frosting to a piping bag fitted with a large star tip and pipe the frosting onto the cupcakes.)

8. Decorate each cupcake with sprinkles. Bright colors contrast well with the frosting, while gold sprinkles give an air of elegance.

INGREDIENT TIP: The coffee intensifies the chocolate flavor but doesn't make the cupcakes taste like coffee. If you don't have coffee or espresso on hand, skip it and increase the amount of milk to 1 cup.

Cinnamon-Peach Whoopie Pies

Makes 6 jumbo or 14 mini whoopie pies

Prep time: 30 minutes   **Bake time:** 15 minutes

The sandwich portion of these whoopie pies is a cross between a hefty cake and a soft baked cookie. It's strong enough to hold the filling but delicate enough to give way to a soft crumb. The star of the show is the marshmallow–cream cheese filling. If you're not eating them right away, store the plain cakes in an airtight container layered between parchment paper and the filling in a separate airtight container in the refrigerator. Assemble just before eating.

For the cakes

8 tablespoons (1 stick, 113g) unsalted butter, at room temperature

1 cup (198g) granulated sugar

¼ cup sour cream

2 large eggs

1 teaspoon vanilla extract

2 cups (240g) all-purpose flour

1 teaspoon baking powder

½ teaspoon baking soda

½ teaspoon salt

1. Preheat the oven to 350°F. Line two rimmed baking sheets with parchment paper.

2. In a medium bowl, use a hand mixer on medium speed to whip the butter, granulated sugar, and sour cream until light and fluffy. Scrape down the sides of the bowl as needed.

3. Add the eggs and vanilla and whip on high speed for a full minute. Scrape down the sides of the bowl. Add the flour, baking powder, baking soda, and salt and whip for another 30 seconds to combine.

4. For jumbo sandwiches, use a ¼-cup measuring up to make 12 cake halves. Place 6 scoops on each baking sheet, spaced 3 to 4 inches apart. To make mini sandwiches, use a 2-tablespoon measuring spoon to make 28 cake halves. Place 14 scoops on each baking sheet, spaced 2 inches apart.

5. Bake the jumbo sandwiches for about 15 minutes or the mini sandwiches for 10 to 12 minutes, until they are golden around the edges and easily peel away from the parchment paper. Let cool.

For the filling

1 (8-ounce) package cream cheese, at room temperature

1½ cups (170g) powdered sugar

1 teaspoon ground cinnamon

Pinch salt

1 teaspoon vanilla extract

1 (7-ounce) container marshmallow crème

2 ripe peaches, pitted and thinly sliced

6. While the cakes are baking, wash and dry the bowl and mixer attachments. Using the hand mixer, cream the cream cheese until no lumps are visible, scraping down the sides of the bowl as needed. Add the powdered sugar, cinnamon, salt, and vanilla and mix until combined. Scrape down the sides of the bowl and add the marshmallow crème. Mix on high speed to fully incorporate. The filling might be very soft. Refrigerate until ready to fill the sandwiches.

7. To assemble, scoop a dollop of filling onto one cake and spread it to the edges. Add a layer of sliced peaches on top of the filling and top with another cake. Serve.

VARIATION TIP: I love these whoopie pies with peaches, but they're also delicious with strawberries, blueberries, or raspberries. If using berries, swap the cinnamon for an equal amount of grated lemon zest.

Skillet Pineapple Upside-Down Cake

Serves 8

Prep time: 15 minutes   **Bake time:** 45 minutes

The 1950s called and they want their dessert back—but I'm not giving it up. Fruit and cake that makes its own sticky glaze? Sign me up. The rum is my own addition. I enjoy this cake served warm with ice cream on top.

4 tablespoons (½ stick, 56g) unsalted butter, at room temperature, plus 4 tablespoons (½ stick, 56g) unsalted butter, melted

1 cup (213g) plus ½ packed cup (106g) brown sugar, divided

¾ cup pineapple juice from the can, divided

2 tablespoons plus ½ cup dark rum

¼ cup vegetable oil

3 large eggs

2 cups (240g) all-purpose flour

1½ teaspoons baking powder

½ teaspoon baking soda

½ teaspoon salt

½ teaspoon ground cinnamon

1 teaspoon vanilla extract

6 canned pineapple rings

1. Preheat the oven to 350°F.

2. Combine 4 tablespoons room temperature butter, ½ cup brown sugar, ¼ cup pineapple juice, and 2 tablespoons dark rum in a 9-inch ovenproof skillet. Whisk lightly to combine and place in the oven for 5 minutes as it preheats, then set aside.

3. In a medium bowl, combine 4 tablespoons melted butter the oil, 1 cup brown sugar, and the eggs. Whisk until no egg streaks remain.

4. Add 1 cup flour; whisk until combined. Add the remaining 1 cup flour, the baking powder, baking soda, salt, and cinnamon; whisk until just combined. Whisk in the remaining ½ cup pineapple juice, ½ cup rum, and the vanilla.

5. Place as many pineapple rings as you can fit into the bottom of the skillet. Pour the batter into the skillet.

6. Bake for 45 minutes, or until the cake center springs back when lightly pressed.

7. Let cool. Invert the cake onto a plate. If any pineapple rings stick to the pan, just put them back in place. Serve warm or at room temperature.

Chocolate Chunk Pound Cake

Makes 1 large loaf

Prep time: 15 minutes   **Bake time:** 1 hour 30 minutes

I've always been fascinated by pound cake. Pound cake gets its name from its original recipe: 1 pound each of sugar, flour, butter, and eggs. That's a 4-pound dessert! You've got to respect that. This version deviates from the classic with a hint of brown sugar, a healthy dose of vanilla extract, and chocolate chunks. This dense cake bakes low and slow, so be patient. Serve it with fruit and whipped cream, or toast a slice with butter and hope nobody is watching.

Nonstick cooking spray (optional)

8 tablespoons (1 stick, 113g) unsalted butter, at room temperature

1 cup (198g) granulated sugar

½ packed cup (106g) brown sugar

1 cup sour cream

1 tablespoon vanilla extract

3 large eggs

2 cups (240g) all-purpose flour

½ teaspoon baking soda

½ teaspoon salt

1 cup (170g) chocolate chunks

VARIATION TIP: If you don't have a large loaf pan, a smaller one will work. Add the batter about two-thirds of the way up the pan. The remaining batter can be baked in muffin tins.

1. Preheat the oven to 300°F. Grease a 10-by-5-inch loaf pan with nonstick spray or line it with a parchment-paper sling (see Technique tip on page 47).

2. In a medium bowl, using a hand mixer, cream the butter, granulated sugar, and brown sugar until light and fluffy, 2 to 3 minutes. Scrape down the sides and bottom of the bowl periodically.

3. Add the sour cream, vanilla, and 1 egg, mixing until combined. Add the remaining 2 eggs, one at a time, mixing between each addition. Add the flour, baking soda, and salt and mix until fully incorporated.

4. Using a spatula, fold in the chocolate chunks.

5. Pour the batter into the loaf pan; it's thick, so you will need to coax the batter into the bottom and corners.

6. Bake for 1 hour 30 minutes, or until the cake is golden on top and firm to the touch, and a toothpick inserted into the center comes out clean.

Bourbon-Vanilla Bundt Cake

Serves 12

Prep time: 15 minutes   **Bake time:** 55 minutes

This cake is studded with vanilla bean specks, and the oak and caramel notes of the bourbon dance beautifully in this cake. The lightly sweet notes are perfect for an adult birthday cake. Serve with sliced strawberries and whipped cream.

Nonstick cooking spray

1¼ cups (150g) all-purpose flour, plus more for dusting

8 tablespoons (1 stick, 113g) unsalted butter, at room temperature

1½ cups (297g) granulated sugar

½ cup sour cream

2 large eggs

1 teaspoon baking powder

½ teaspoon baking soda

½ teaspoon salt

1 cup milk

1 cup (120g) cake flour

1 tablespoon vanilla extract

1 vanilla bean, halved lengthwise, seeds scraped out (see Ingredient tip)

⅓ cup bourbon (such as Henry McKenna)

Powdered sugar, for dusting

1. Preheat the oven to 350°F. Spray a Bundt pan with cooking spray and lightly dust it with flour.

2. In a medium bowl, using a hand mixer, cream the butter, granulated sugar, and sour cream until light and fluffy. Mix in the eggs, scraping down the sides of the bowl as needed.

3. Add the all-purpose flour, baking powder, baking soda, and salt and mix to combine. Add ½ cup milk and continue mixing. Add the cake flour and the remaining ½ cup milk and mix to combine. Stir in the vanilla extract, vanilla bean seeds, and bourbon. Pour the batter into the pan and smooth the top with a spatula.

4. Bake for 55 minutes, or until the center springs back when lightly touched.

5. Let cool. Top the cake with a dusting of powdered sugar.

INGREDIENT TIP: To prepare the vanilla bean, use a sharp knife to carefully cut the bean in half lengthwise. Using the tip of the knife, press down the length of one half of the bean, scraping as you go. The vanilla bean "caviar" will collect on the side of the knife. Repeat with the other length.

VARIATION TIP: Want a different flavor combination? Add 1 teaspoon of pumpkin pie spice and replace the bourbon with spiced rum for spiced rum cake.

Red Velvet Lava Cakes

Makes 8 individual cakes

Prep time: 10 minutes **Bake time:** 12 minutes

These lava cakes are super simple to make but end up way fancier than suggested by the effort required. These are best served warm but can be made ahead and baked when you need them—try topping them with berries and whipped cream.

4 tablespoons (½ stick, 56g) unsalted butter, at room temperature, plus 10 tablespoons (1¼ sticks, 142g) unsalted butter

¼ cup (49g) granulated sugar

⅓ cup (57g) chopped bittersweet or semisweet chocolate

1 cup (170g) chopped white chocolate

3 large eggs

3 large egg yolks

1½ cups (170g) powdered sugar

½ cup (60g) all-purpose flour

1 teaspoon vanilla extract

1 tablespoon white vinegar

½ teaspoon salt

Few drops red food coloring

2 tablespoons vanilla liqueur (such as Baileys vanilla-cinnamon) or vanilla vodka (optional)

1. Preheat the oven to 425°F.

2. Using the 4 tablespoons room-temperature butter, generously grease eight 4-ounce ramekins. Sprinkle the granulated sugar in each and tilt it around to cover the sides and bottom of the ramekins. Pour out any extra sugar. Set aside.

3. In a medium microwave-safe bowl, melt the bittersweet and white chocolate with the remaining 10 tablespoons butter in the microwave in 30-second increments, whisking in between and until fully incorporated. Allow the mixture to cool slightly.

4. Once slightly cooled, mix in the eggs and egg yolks. Mix in the powdered sugar, flour, vanilla, vinegar, salt, food coloring, and liqueur (if using). Divide the batter evenly between the ramekins.

5. Bake for 12 minutes. The center should still be jiggly, but the edges will be just set.

6. While they're still hot, invert each cake onto a plate. Serve warm.

Butter Pecan–Dulce de Leche Coffee Cake

Serves 9

Prep time: 20 minutes   **Bake time:** 35 to 40 minutes

I don't know about you, but in the mornings, I just want my coffee and a small sweet bite of something. I've never been a savory morning person, and I don't need a full meal. This coffee cake has my name all over it. With warmth from the brown sugar, cinnamon, and dulce de leche and a lovely crunch from the toasted pecans, I could eat this every morning—and twice on Sunday.

For the cake batter

Nonstick cooking spray
   (optional)
8 tablespoons (1 stick;
   113g) unsalted butter, at
   room temperature
1 packed cup (213g)
   brown sugar
¾ cup sour cream
2 large eggs
1½ cups (180g)
   all-purpose flour
1 teaspoon baking powder
½ teaspoon baking soda
½ teaspoon salt
1 cup canned dulce
   de leche

1. Preheat the oven to 350°F. Line an 8-inch square pan with parchment paper or mist it with nonstick cooking spray.

2. Using a microwave-safe medium bowl and a hand mixer, cream the butter and brown sugar until light and fluffy.

3. Beat in the sour cream, scraping down the sides of the bowl as needed. The mixture may appear runny, but this is normal.

4. Add the eggs one at a time, mixing between additions. Add the flour, baking powder, baking soda, and salt and mix until incorporated.

5. Transfer half of the batter to the pan and smooth the top with a spatula.

For the streusel

4 tablespoons (½ stick, 56g) unsalted butter
¼ packed cup (53g) brown sugar
1 tablespoon ground cinnamon
1 cup (120g) all-purpose flour
½ cup (57g) roughly chopped pecans

6. Pour the dulce de leche over the top and carefully smooth it out across the batter. Cover it with the remaining batter and smooth it into an even layer.

7. Rinse out the medium bowl to make the streusel. Melt the butter in the microwave. Sprinkle the brown sugar over the top and stir with a fork. Stir in the cinnamon and flour. The mixture will be lumpy. Fold in the pecans.

8. Sprinkle the streusel mixture over the top of the cake batter, using your fingers to break up any big clumps into smaller ones.

9. Bake for 35 to 40 minutes, until the center of the cake is firm. Serve warm or at room temperature.

SUBSTITUTION TIP: If you have a nut allergy, simply leave out the pecans. But don't skip the streusel—it's a must!

Orange Creamsicle Poke Cake

Serves 12

Prep time: 20 minutes   **Bake time:** 40 minutes

This cake is best served cold to replicate the flavors of that classic orange-vanilla frozen treat. The orange soda is poured over the top for a delicious soaked cake reminiscent of a tres leches cake. If you close your eyes, you can pretend you're a kid again, sitting on the porch with an ice pop dripping down your hand.

For the cake

Nonstick cooking spray

8 tablespoons (1 stick, 113g) unsalted butter, at room temperature

1 cup (198g) granulated sugar

5 large eggs

2 teaspoons vanilla extract

1¼ cups (150g) all-purpose flour

1 teaspoon baking powder

½ teaspoon salt

For the glaze

1 cup orange soda

½ cup heavy (whipping) cream

1 (14-ounce) can sweetened condensed milk

1. Preheat the oven to 325°F. Spray a 9-by-13-inch baking pan with nonstick spray.

2. In a medium bowl, using a hand mixer, combine the butter and granulated sugar until light and fluffy. Add the eggs one at a time, mixing well after each addition. Mix in the vanilla, scraping down the sides of the bowl. Add the flour, baking powder, and salt and mix until just combined. Pour the batter into the baking pan.

3. Bake for 40 minutes, or until the center springs back when lightly touched.

4. While the cake bakes, make the glaze. In a measuring cup, combine the soda, heavy cream, and sweetened condensed milk. Whisk to combine. Set aside.

5. When the cake comes out of the oven and while it is still warm, use a skewer to poke holes in the cake. Pour the glaze over it. I recommend doing this in 3 batches, letting the cake absorb the glaze slowly between batches.

For the frosting

8 tablespoons (1 stick, 113g) unsalted butter, at room temperature

1 (8-ounce) package cream cheese, at room temperature

¼ teaspoon salt

1 teaspoon vanilla extract

3 cups (405g) powdered sugar

2 tablespoons milk

6. Once the cake has cooled to room temperature, transfer the cake to the refrigerator. Wash and dry the bowl to make the frosting.

7. Once the cake is completely chilled, using a hand mixer on medium speed, beat the butter and cream cheese until fluffy. Mix in the salt and vanilla. Add the powdered sugar 1 cup at a time. As it becomes very stiff and difficult to mix, add the milk. Mix until the frosting is light and fluffy. Frost the top of the cake.

8. Serve this cake chilled for the best flavor. The cake can be made 1 to 2 days in advance and stored, covered, in the refrigerator.

Pistachio Layer Cake with Cherry Frosting

Serves 12

Prep time: 1 hour, plus cooling and chilling   **Bake time:** 20 to 25 minutes

I paired this soft pistachio cake with a maraschino cherry frosting. Normally I love fresh (real) fruit in my baked goods, but this is probably one of my favorite uses for maraschino cherries. They work especially well with the pistachio.

For the cake

Nonstick cooking spray

¼ cup (35g) shelled pistachios

2 cups (440g) granulated sugar

1¾ cups (218g) all-purpose flour

¾ cup (94g) cake flour

1 (¼-cup, 50g) packet powdered instant pistachio pudding mix

1½ teaspoons baking powder

1 teaspoon baking soda

1 teaspoon salt

2 cups milk

½ cup vegetable oil

2 large eggs

1. Preheat the oven to 350°F. Spray three 8-inch round cake pans with nonstick spray. Line the bottom of each with parchment-paper circles.

2. Chop the pistachios into small pieces or place them in a sandwich bag and smash with a rolling pin until broken up. Set aside.

3. In a medium bowl, combine the sugar, all-purpose flour, cake flour, pudding mix, baking powder, baking soda, and salt and whisk to combine. Add the milk, oil, and eggs and whisk until there are no lumps. Fold in the pistachios.

4. Divide the batter equally among the three pans.

5. Bake for 20 to 25 minutes, until the center springs back when lightly touched and the edges start to pull away from the pan.

6. Allow the cakes to cool completely in the pans.

7. Wash and dry the bowl to make the frosting. Using a hand mixer, whip the butter, shortening, salt, and vanilla on low speed until incorporated. Scrape down the sides of the bowl, then increase the mixer speed to medium-high and beat for 3 minutes, or until the mixture is light and fluffy. It should almost double in volume.

For the frosting

8 tablespoons (1 stick, 113g) unsalted butter, at room temperature

½ cup vegetable shortening

1 teaspoon salt

½ teaspoon vanilla extract

4 cups (454g) powdered sugar, sifted if lumpy

1 to 2 tablespoons maraschino cherry juice

½ cup roughly chopped maraschino cherries

8. Reduce the mixer's speed to low. Add the powdered sugar in three additions, mixing fully between additions and scraping down the sides of the bowl as needed. Add the cherry juice, 1 tablespoon at a time, to achieve a spreadable consistency. The frosting should be smooth, light, and fluffy. Mix in the chopped cherries.

9. Remove the cooled cakes from their pans and peel away the parchment paper from their bottoms. If the top of the cake layers have a dome, slice that portion off with a serrated bread knife. Place the first cake layer faceup on a plate. Place about ½ cup of frosting on the layer and, using an offset spatula, smooth the frosting across the top of the cake to the edges. Place the second cake layer facedown over the frosting and add ½ cup of frosting. Smooth the frosting across the cake to the edges, then place the final cake facedown so that you have the flat bottom on top. Smooth another ½ cup of frosting over the top of the cake in an even layer.

10. Refrigerate the cake for 30 minutes. This will set the crumb coat and help you have a better-looking final coat of frosting. (Leave the frosting out so it will stay spreadable.)

11. After about 30 minutes, smooth a final thin layer of frosting over the top of the cake, creating a "naked cake" look. This cake can be made up to 1 day in advance; simply store it in a covered cake container at room temperature to keep it from drying out.

Blood Orange-Ricotta Cake

Serves 12

Prep time: 20 minutes   **Bake time:** 40 minutes

Do you ever find yourself late to the game on all the best things? That was me with blood oranges. This slightly sweeter, less-acidic orange makes all the difference in this cake. While they're in season, I recommend zesting and juicing a few and freezing to make this cake at other times in the year. You'll thank me, I promise.

Gluten-free nonstick
  cooking spray
8 tablespoons (1 stick,
  113g) unsalted butter, at
  room temperature
1⅓ cups (264g) granulated
  sugar
4 large eggs
1 cup (227g) ricotta cheese
2½ cups (240g)
  almond flour
2 tablespoons cornstarch
½ teaspoon baking soda
½ teaspoon salt
Grated zest and juice of
  2 blood oranges
⅓ cup (38g) sliv-
  ered almonds
3 tablespoons
  demerara sugar

1. Preheat the oven to 325°F. Grease a 10-inch round cake pan with nonstick spray.

2. In a medium bowl, using a hand mixer, cream the butter and granulated sugar until fluffy. Add the eggs, one at a time, mixing between additions and scraping the sides of the bowl as necessary. Stir in the ricotta cheese.

3. Add the almond flour, cornstarch, baking soda, and salt and stir. Finally, stir in the orange zest and juice. Pour the batter into the cake pan and smooth out the top. Sprinkle the almonds and demerara sugar over the top.

4. Bake for 40 minutes, or until the top is golden and the center is set. This cake is very moist, so it will have a slightly wet crumb when finished.

5. Allow the cake to cool completely, then store it in an airtight container at room temperature for up to 3 days.

Sprinkle Roll Cake

Serves 8

Prep time: 10 minutes, plus 30 minutes to chill   **Bake time:** 20 to 25 minutes

Roll cakes have always intimidated me a bit, but they're actually easy. The thing to remember is to roll the cake while it's still warm and handle it carefully. Be sure to roll this cake with the bottom side out so that you can see the sprinkles.

3 large eggs

¾ cup (148g) granulated sugar

2 tablespoons vegetable oil

¾ cup (94g) all-purpose flour

½ cup (60g) cake flour

1 teaspoon baking powder

½ teaspoon salt

2 tablespoons sprinkles

½ cup jam of your choice (I like raspberry)

2 cups frozen whipped topping, thawed

Powdered sugar, for dusting

VARIATION TIP: Switch out your fillings for endless dessert variations—grape jelly and peanut butter whipped cream would be delightful.

1. Preheat the oven to 350°F. Line a 9-by-13-inch pan or quarter sheet pan with parchment.

2. In a medium bowl, using a hand mixer, whip the eggs and granulated sugar until light and airy, 2 to 3 minutes. Add the oil, both flours, baking powder, salt, and sprinkles and mix until just combined (don't overmix.) Spread the batter into the prepared pan and smooth the top.

3. Bake for 20 to 25 minutes. The top should be lightly golden and not sticky to the touch.

4. Allow the cake to cool slightly, just enough that you can handle it. Turn the cake out onto a clean dish towel. Flip the cake back over, so that the parchment-paper on the bottom of the cake is on the towel. Using the towel to help, start on the long side of the cake and carefully roll it up. This will make it so the smooth bottom of the cake is on the outside.

5. Refrigerate the rolled-up cake and towel until completely cooled, about 30 minutes. Carefully unroll the cake and spread the curved inside with the jam and whipped topping. Roll up the cake over the jam and whipped topping, peeling the parchment paper off as you go. Place the cake seam-side down on a serving tray. Dust with powdered sugar.

Baked Alaska Bowl

Serves 10

Prep time: 20 minutes, plus 4 hours to chill   **Bake time:** 45 minutes

Baked Alaska is one of those throwback desserts that does not get enough love. Cake? Good. Ice cream? Good. Toasted meringue? Good. All together? So good! This recipe works best with a kitchen torch, but you can make it work with the broil setting on your oven (carefully) or just leave a pristine white meringue on top. This recipe goes from counter to oven in the same bowl, and then we use the bowl again for the meringue.

For the cake

**4 tablespoons
  (½ stick, 56g) unsalted
  butter, melted**
**1 cup (198g) granulated
  sugar**
½ cup vegetable oil
**½ cup (42g) unsweetened
  natural cocoa powder**
**2 cups (240g)
  all-purpose flour**
1 teaspoon baking powder
½ teaspoon baking soda
½ teaspoon salt
1 cup buttermilk
**1 quart ice cream of your
  choice (I like vanilla–
  chocolate chip)**

1. Preheat oven to 350°F.

2. In a medium, ovenproof metal bowl (about 3 quarts in size), whisk together the butter, sugar, oil, and cocoa until combined. Add the flour, baking powder, baking soda, salt, and buttermilk. Whisk until no lumps remain.

3. Place the bowl in the oven. Bake for 45 minutes. If the center is not quite set, that's okay. The edges should be baked and firm at least 1 inch around the sides of the bowl.

4. Allow the cake to cool enough to be handled. Use a knife to cut a circle in the center of the cake for the ice cream, leaving at least 2 inches of cake around the edges. Scoop out the center of the cake (snacking on this is encouraged). Once the cake is completely cooled, remove the ice cream from the freezer to thaw a bit.

5. Using a knife, gently go around the inside edge of the bowl to help remove the cake. Flip the bowl upside down to release the cake onto a plate.

For the meringue

4 large egg whites
**1 cup (198g) granu-
lated sugar**

6. Wash and dry the bowl and line it with plastic wrap. Return the cake to the bowl. Fill the center of the cake with the ice cream. Place the bowl in the freezer to set, about 4 hours.

7. Once the cake and ice cream are set, invert it onto a plate and place the plastic-wrapped cake back in the freezer.

8. To make the meringue, pour an inch or two of water into a medium pot and heat over medium heat. Nestle the bowl in the pot, making sure the bowl does not touch the water. Add the egg whites and sugar. As the water heats, using a whisk or hand mixer on low speed, beat until the sugar dissolves. Once the sugar melts, remove the bowl from the heat. Turn the hand mixer to high and beat until stiff peaks form, 5 to 7 minutes.

9. Remove the cake from the freezer and remove the plastic wrap. Using a spatula, cover the cake with the meringue. Serve as-is, or, if you have a kitchen torch, carefully toasting the meringue until it is golden. Alternatively, preheat the oven to broil on high. Place the cake in the oven until the meringue is golden (watch with the door open), no more than 1 minute so the ice cream doesn't melt.

10. Slice and serve immediately. Although the meringue can go in the freezer, it's not as tasty.

Strawberry Angel Shortcake

Serves 10

Prep time: 15 minutes   **Bake time:** 35 minutes

Angel food cake is so much fun to eat—it's springy and light, like eating a slice of sweetened air. Paired with fresh strawberries and cream, this is a delightful dessert that simply screams spring. It requires a tube pan, which is not the same as a Bundt pan.

1½ cups egg whites (12 to 15 large egg whites, freshly cracked)
2 cups (227g) powdered sugar, divided
1 cup (120g) cake flour
2 tablespoons cornstarch
1 teaspoon salt
2 teaspoons vanilla extract
2 cups frozen whipped topping, thawed
1 quart strawberries, hulled and sliced

1. Place an oven rack in the lower two-thirds of the oven. Preheat to 350°F.

2. In a medium bowl, using a hand mixer, mix the egg whites and 1 cup powdered sugar on high speed for 10 minutes, or until the egg whites have doubled in volume and hold a soft peak (when you pull out the mixer, the peak droops slightly).

3. Add the remaining 1 cup powdered sugar, the cake flour, cornstarch, salt, and vanilla. Using a spatula, fold in the ingredients by hand until just combined. You don't want to overmix the batter and lose the air whipped into the egg whites. Pour the batter into an ungreased tube pan and smooth the top of the batter.

4. Bake for 35 minutes, or until the cake is lightly golden, it springs back to the touch, and it has a matte, not glossy, appearance.

5. Turn the cake pan upside down and allow the cake to cool this way. If it cools right-side-up, the cake will fall in on itself.

6. Once cool, gently run a knife around the inside edge of the pan, including around the tube. Invert the cake onto a plate to remove it from the pan. Halve the cake crosswise with a serrated bread knife. Spread the whipped topping over the bottom half and cover with sliced berries. Place the other half of the cake on top. Serve sliced, with more berries.

7. Loosely wrap the cake in plastic wrap and store in the refrigerator up to 2 days.

INGREDIENT TIP: This cake needs freshly cracked egg whites. You might be tempted to use purchased egg whites, but you won't get the lift an angel food cake relies on, as there is no other leavener used to make it.

Chapter 5

Cobblers, Puddings, and Fruity Desserts

This chapter highlights the versatility of desserts; there are warm desserts, like the Honey-Mango Bread Pudding (page 82) that will change how you look at Hawaiian rolls, and decadent treats like a Cheesecake Napoleon (page 84). I can't really pick a favorite because each is uniquely delicious, but they all start with just one bowl.

Cheesecake Napoleon
page 84

Blueberry Buckle

Serves 8

Prep time: 10 minutes   **Bake time:** 45 minutes

What's the difference between a crisp, a crumble, a cobbler, and a buckle? Both a crisp and a crumble are fruit desserts topped with streusel, but crisps use oats. Cobblers are fruit served with a biscuit-like topping, and buckles are fruit topped with cake. This buckle comes together quickly and best of all, it's served warm, so no need to wait before enjoying.

2 cups blueberries

8 tablespoons (1 stick, 113g) unsalted butter

1 cup (198g) granulated sugar

2 large eggs

1½ cups (180g) all-purpose flour

1 teaspoon baking powder

½ teaspoon salt

Grated zest and juice of 1 lemon

½ cup milk

¼ cup (20g) sliced almonds

1 tablespoon demerara sugar

Ice cream or whipped cream, for serving

1. Preheat the oven to 350°F.

2. Scatter the blueberries in a 9-inch oven-proof skillet.

3. In a medium microwave-safe bowl, melt the butter in the microwave. Let cool slightly, then whisk in the sugar. Add the eggs one at a time, whisking between each addition, then whisk in the flour, baking powder, and salt until combined.

4. Add the lemon zest, juice, and milk and whisk until the batter is smooth with no lumps.

5. Scrape the batter into the skillet, being careful not to disturb the blueberries too much; Using a spatula, smooth out the top. Sprinkle the sliced almonds and demerara sugar over the top.

6. Bake for 45 minutes, or until the center is set and springs back slightly when pressed. The top will crack and (wait for it) buckle.

7. Serve warm with ice cream or whipped cream.

SUBSTITUTION TIP: Fresh blueberries are best, but frozen will work, too. I love lemon and blueberry together, but strawberries or blackberries would be amazing as well.

Lime-Raspberry Pie

Serves 8

Prep time: 10 minutes, plus 2 hours to chill **Bake time:** 20 minutes

I love a key lime pie. What I don't love is trying to zest and juice those little buggers. As far as I'm concerned, regular limes are just as good, and in this recipe, you need only two good-size ones. Using a premade graham cracker crust takes this pie from craving to finished in 30 minutes. The only hard part will be waiting for it to chill.

Heaping ½ cup (75g) raspberries, plus more for garnish

1 (9-inch) store-bought or homemade graham cracker crust

1 (14-ounce) can sweetened condensed milk

3 large egg yolks

1 tablespoon grated lime zest

½ cup freshly squeezed lime juice

¼ cup heavy (whipping) cream

¼ teaspoon salt

Green food coloring (optional)

TECHNIQUE TIP: To get the most juice out of your limes, roll them on the counter, pressing hard to break up all the little juice capsules inside.

1. Preheat the oven to 325°F.

2. Evenly spread the raspberries in the bottom of the graham cracker crust, so that every slice of pie will have berries studded throughout.

3. In a medium bowl, combine the sweetened condensed milk, egg yolks, lime zest, juice, heavy cream, and salt. Whisk until fully combined. If using the food coloring, add a drop or two at a time until your desired color is achieved. This pie doesn't change color much after baking, so the filling now is what it will look like baked.

4. Pour the filling into the crust, covering the berries. If needed, use a spatula to smooth the top.

5. Bake for 20 minutes. The center will have a slight jiggle when done.

6. Let cool slightly, then chill in the refrigerator for 2 hours before serving. Garnish each slice with additional raspberries. Store leftovers, covered, in the refrigerator for up to 5 days.

SUBSTITUTION TIP: Blackberries are also phenomenal in this pie.

Honey-Mango Bread Pudding

Serves 9

Prep time: 15 minutes   **Bake time:** 45 to 50 minutes

When bread pudding comes to mind, I think of a rich, heavy dessert loaded with spices. This version has a light, tropical feel, thanks to Hawaiian-style bread and a splash of rum. So kick back and pretend you're on an extended vacation.

Nonstick cooking spray

1 (12-ounce) can full-fat coconut milk

⅓ cup honey

2 large eggs

2 tablespoons dark rum

2 tablespoons unsalted butter, melted

10 Hawaiian-style mini rolls or similar sweet-style bread (270g), cut into 1-inch chunks

1 cup diced mango (fresh or frozen)

½ cup heavy (whipping) cream

1½ cups (235g) chopped white chocolate

1. Preheat the oven to 375°F. Lightly grease an 8-inch square baking pan with nonstick spray.

2. In a medium microwave-safe bowl, whisk together the coconut milk, honey, eggs, rum, and butter. Add the bread and mango to the milk mixture and soak for 5 minutes. Stir twice while it soaks to make sure everything is well coated.

3. Transfer the bread mixture to the baking pan. If there is extra liquid, discard it.

4. Bake for 45 to 50 minutes, until the pudding has a slight jiggle but does not look wet. If you prefer the pudding to be really set, move it to the lowest rack on your oven and bake for 10 minutes more.

5. Wash and dry the bowl. Heat the heavy cream in the microwave for 30 seconds, or until it begins to bubble at the edges. Add the white chocolate. Allow to sit for 1 minute, then stir to combine. Microwave for 15 seconds more if any lumps remain, then stir until smooth.

6. Serve the bread pudding warm with the white chocolate glaze spooned over it. Store leftovers covered in the refrigerator for up to 5 days. Reheat before serving.

Baked Peaches

Serves 4

Prep time: 5 minutes **Bake time:** 30 minutes

When peaches are in season, this is hands-down one of the most delicious and shock-ingly simple desserts you can make. Serve warm with ice cream or whipped cream for a fruity, crunchy, slightly sweet treat. It's the perfect end to a meal on a warm summer day.

2 ripe peaches, unpeeled, halved crosswise and pitted

4 tablespoons (½ stick, 56g) unsalted butter, at room temperature

⅔ cup (80g) all-purpose flour

½ packed cup (106g) brown sugar

⅓ cup (30g) old-fashioned rolled oats

½ teaspoon salt

1 teaspoon ground cinnamon

Pinch freshly grated nutmeg

1. Preheat the oven to 350°F. Line a rimmed baking sheet with parchment paper. Roll up four pieces of aluminum foil to form four peach-size rings to hold the peach halves steady.

2. Place the peaches cut-side up on the baking sheet, held in place by the foil rings.

3. In a small bowl, combine the butter, flour, sugar, oats, salt, cinnamon, and nutmeg and mix with a fork to combine.

4. Sprinkle the mixture evenly over the peaches and lightly pack it down over the top.

5. Bake for 30 minutes, or until the crumble mixture is golden and the peaches are soft. Serve warm.

VARIATION TIP: If it's not obvious by now, I really adore the crunch and flavor that nuts add to desserts. I often add about ¼ cup of chopped pecans to this mixture.

Cheesecake Napoleon

Serves 12

Prep time: 30 minutes, plus 3 hours to chill **Bake time:** 1 hour 30 minutes

It's entirely true that I have several "favorite desserts," so if you see me say it more than once, just know that the list is very long. Of course, I am a fan of cheesecake, and although I love the thick New York–style cheesecake I traditionally make, I can't get over the church buffet version I grew up eating, topped with those bright-red, sweet canned cherries. Call it a guilty pleasure. This version combines a baked cheesecake, cherry filling, and crispy puff pastry.

1 (17.3-ounce) package frozen puff pastry, thawed overnight in the refrigerator

¾ cup (148g) granulated sugar

2 (8-ounce) packages cream cheese, at room temperature

2 large eggs

1 large egg yolk

½ cup sour cream

1 teaspoon salt

½ cup heavy (whipping) cream

Grated zest and juice of 1 lemon

1 (15-ounce) can cherry pie filling

1. Preheat the oven to 400°F. Line an 8-inch square baking pan with parchment paper. Line a rimmed baking sheet pan with parchment paper, too, and have a second baking sheet handy.

2. On a clean workspace, roll one puff pastry sheet into an 8-by-12-inch rectangle. Using a sharp knife or pizza cutter, cut it into one 8-inch square and one 4-by-8-inch rectangle. Repeat with the second sheet of puff pastry. (The two rectangles will be used to make a third square.)

3. Place two pastry squares on the parchment paper–lined baking sheet and place another sheet of parchment paper on top. Place the second baking sheet on top of the parchment paper; this keeps the pastry from puffing up too much while it bakes. Bake for 10 minutes, then remove the top baking sheet pan and the top layer of parchment paper and bake for 5 minutes more. Repeat the process to bake the two small rectangles that will form a square.

4. While the puff pastry bakes, in a medium bowl using a hand mixer, cream the sugar and cream cheese until light and fluffy. Add the eggs and egg yolk, one at a time, mixing between additions and scraping down the sides of the bowl as necessary. Mix in the sour cream and salt. Add the heavy cream and continue to beat, starting at low speed and ending up on high speed, to add volume. Mix in the lemon zest and juice.

5. Reduce the oven temperature to 350°F. Place one baked puff pastry square in the 8-inch pan. Top with half of the cheesecake mixture, then dot with as much cherry pie filling as you like. Place the two small baked rectangles of puff pastry side by side in the pan, then cover with the remaining cheesecake filling and more cherry pie filling. Top with the other baked puff pastry square.

6. Bake for 1 hour, or until the top is golden and feels firm.

7. Let cool, then refrigerate until chilled through, about 3 hours. Store leftovers, covered, in the refrigerator, for up to 3 days.

VARIATION TIP: Sprinkle the puff pastry with ground cinnamon and sugar before baking for added flavor.

Brownie-Cheesecake Pie

Serves 12

Prep time: 45 minutes, plus 4 hours to chill **Bake time:** 50 minutes

There is something irresistible about the combination of rich chocolate paired with the tanginess of cheesecake. This recipe takes all that and adds the element of a crisp crust. This pie takes a traditionally handheld brownie-cheesecake dessert and elevates it to a plated masterpiece.

For the brownie filling

- **4 ounces (113g) dark chocolate, roughly chopped**
- **8 tablespoons (1 stick, 113g) unsalted butter, at room temperature**
- **2 tablespoons Dutch-process cocoa powder**
- **1 teaspoon vanilla extract**
- **½ cup (99g) granulated sugar**
- **½ packed cup (100g) light brown sugar**
- **2 large eggs**
- **¾ cup (94g) all-purpose flour**
- **½ teaspoon salt**
- **½ teaspoon baking powder**
- **1 (9-inch) store-bought piecrust**

1. Preheat the oven to 350°F.

2. In a medium microwave-safe bowl, combine the chocolate, butter, cocoa powder, and vanilla. Microwave in 30-second increments, stirring in between, until the chocolate is melted and smooth.

3. Add the granulated sugar and brown sugar and stir to combine. Add the eggs one at a time, mixing between additions. Add the flour, salt, and baking powder and mix until the batter is smooth. Pour the batter into the piecrust. If you scrape out the bowl well with a silicone spatula, there's no need to wash it, just move on to the cheesecake.

4. In the same bowl, whisk together the cream cheese and sugar until no lumps are visible. Whisk in the egg, followed by the heavy cream, vanilla, and salt.

For the cheesecake

1 (8-ounce) package cream cheese, at room temperature

⅓ cup (67g) granulated sugar

1 large egg

¼ cup heavy (whipping) cream

1 teaspoon vanilla extract

¼ teaspoon salt

5. Drop scoops of cheesecake filling over the brownie batter, marbling it with the spoon as you go. Lightly smooth the top.

6. Bake for about 50 minutes, until the edges are set, the center has a slight jiggle, and the top is firm to the touch.

7. Let cool, then chill in the refrigerator for at least 4 hours; overnight is best. Serve cold.

Peanut Butter and Jelly Cobbler

Serves 9

Prep time: 15 minutes　　**Bake time:** 40 minutes

There are few foods that truly transcend everything to be a "perfect food," and yet, as simple as it may be, fresh white bread topped with peanut butter and chilled jelly fits into that category. This cobbler is super soft with a lovely peanut butter bite through-out that's enhanced by a bit of your favorite jelly. While this is meant to be a dessert, I have more than once warmed up a bowl for breakfast. Protein, am I right?

Nonstick cooking spray (optional)

8 tablespoons (1 stick, 113g) unsalted butter, at room temperature

1 cup (198g) granulated sugar

¼ cup creamy peanut butter

1 large egg

1½ cups (180g) all-purpose flour, divided

½ teaspoon salt

½ teaspoon baking powder

½ cup jelly or preserve of your choice (I'm a strawberry fan)

¼ cup chopped salted peanuts

1. Preheat the oven to 350°F. Line an 8-inch square baking pan with parchment paper or spray with nonstick spray.

2. In a medium bowl, using a hand mixer, beat the butter, sugar, and peanut butter until light and fluffy, scraping down the sides of the bowl as needed. Add the egg and continue beating. Add 1 cup flour, the salt, and the baking powder. Mix to combine.

3. Scoop out three-quarters of the dough and press it evenly into the baking pan. Spread the jelly evenly on top.

4. Mix the remaining ½ cup flour into the remaining dough. It should become very crumbly. Mix in the chopped peanuts. Sprinkle the mixture over the top of the jelly layer, using your fingers to break up any large clumps.

5. Bake for 40 minutes, or until the center is set.

6. Serve warm. Wrap the leftovers and store at room temperature. Reheat before serving.

Lemon Custard

Serves 9

Prep time: 10 minutes, plus 4 hours to chill   **Bake time:** 45 minutes

This recipe is a riff on a magic bar. The lemon custard separates into layers as it bakes. The bottom forms a crust, while the top has an almost soufflé-like consistency. There's a lovely lemon flavor throughout. This recipe is equally delicious made with grapefruit.

3 large eggs

1 cup (113g) powdered
   sugar, plus more
   for dusting

8 tablespoons (1 stick,
   113g) unsalted butter, at
   room temperature

1 cup (120g)
   all-purpose flour

¼ teaspoon salt

2 cups milk

Grated zest of 1 lemon

Berries, for serving
   (optional)

1. Preheat the oven to 325°F. Line an 8-inch square baking pan with parchment paper.

2. In a medium bowl, using a hand mixer, combine the eggs, powdered sugar, and butter and whip on high speed until light and fluffy, 3 to 5 minutes. This step is crucial to getting a bit of lift in the custard.

3. Add the flour and salt and mix until just combined. Add the milk and lemon zest and mix until just combined. Pour the custard into the pan.

4. Bake for 45 minutes, or until the edges are golden; the top will have a slight jiggle. Overall, it will be puffed up, but once you take it out, it will fall, so don't be alarmed.

5. Allow to cool for about 15 minutes, then chill in the refrigerator for about 4 hours. Slice and serve dusted with additional powdered sugar and berries, if desired.

VARIATION TIP: I've eaten this dessert both warm and chilled, and it's like experiencing two different desserts. Warm is more like a soufflé and the texture is springier, while chilled it's dense and custardy. Try it both ways and see which you prefer.

Overnight Oatmeal Bake

Serves 8

Prep time: 15 minutes, plus overnight to soak   **Bake time:** 40 minutes

In the morning, if you don't feel like cooking, this bake will be your jam. All you have to do is throw it in the oven. The oats soften in the refrigerator overnight and crisp up when they're baked, transforming into a delicious, fruity breakfast.

2 cups medium-diced fruit and/or berries (fresh or frozen)

2 tablespoons granulated sugar

1 cup almond milk or milk of your choice

¼ cup honey

2 tablespoons unsalted butter, melted

1 large egg

1 teaspoon vanilla extract

¼ teaspoon salt

¼ cup (20g) sliced almonds

1½ cups (140g) old-fashioned rolled oats

3 tablespoons demerara sugar

1. Place the fruit in an 8-inch square baking pan. Sprinkle the granulated sugar over the top.

2. In a medium bowl, whisk together the milk, honey, butter, egg, vanilla, and salt. Add the almonds and oats. Mix to coat the oats completely with the mixture. Carefully pour over the fruit. Do not stir, as the fruit should sit on the bottom. Cover and refrigerate overnight.

3. The next morning, preheat the oven to 350°F.

4. Sprinkle the demerara sugar over the top of the oats. Bake for 40 minutes, or until the mixture no longer appears wet and the oats are toasted.

5. Serve warm. Wrap and refrigerate any left-overs, which can be reheated in the microwave the next day.

VARIATION TIP: Use whatever fruit you like or have on hand. I like a combination of cherries and strawberries with a few blueberries thrown in. During the fall fruit season, add 1 teaspoon of ground cinnamon to the oat mixture and embrace the autumn flavors with apples, pears, and/or figs.

Coconut Pudding Pie

Serves 8

Prep time: 10 minutes, plus 3 hours to chill   **Bake time:** 30 minutes

There are many desserts that combine chocolate, coconut, and almonds, because the flavor combination checks all the boxes: salty, sweet, creamy, and crunchy. This recipe uses canned coconut milk in two places.

1 (12- to 14.5-ounce) can full-fat coconut milk

2 large eggs

1 cup (198g) granulated sugar

4 tablespoons (½ stick, 56g) unsalted butter, melted

1 teaspoon vanilla extract

¼ cup (30g) all-purpose flour

¼ teaspoon baking powder

¼ teaspoon salt

1 cup (85g) sweetened shredded coconut

¼ cup (29g) slivered almonds

1 (9-inch) store-bought piecrust

1 cup (170g) chopped dark chocolate

SUBSTITUTION TIP: If you can't eat nuts, substitute cocoa nibs for the almonds. They provide the same crunchy texture and also up the chocolate flavor.

1. Preheat the oven to 350°F.

2. Open the can of coconut milk carefully without shaking it. It will have two parts: a thick cream that collects at the top and a liquid at the bottom. Use a spoon to scoop out ¼ cup of the thick cream at the top to get to the milk (set the cream aside; it will be used later). Measure out 1 cup liquid coconut milk. If there's not a full cup of milk in the can, add some of the coconut cream until you have 1 cup.

3. In a medium microwave-safe bowl, whisk together the eggs and sugar until well combined. Add the butter, coconut milk, and vanilla and mix well. Add the flour, baking powder, and salt and mix until well combined. Fold in the shredded coconut and almonds. Pour the mixture into the crust.

4. Bake for 30 minutes, or until the crust is golden, the top has a brown and crackled appearance, and the center is set. Set aside to cool.

5. While the pie cools, wash and dry the bowl. In the bowl, combine the reserved coconut cream and chocolate. Microwave in 30-second increments, whisking between each, until the chocolate is melted and smooth. Pour the ganache over the top of the pie. Refrigerate the pie for 2 to 3 hours before serving.

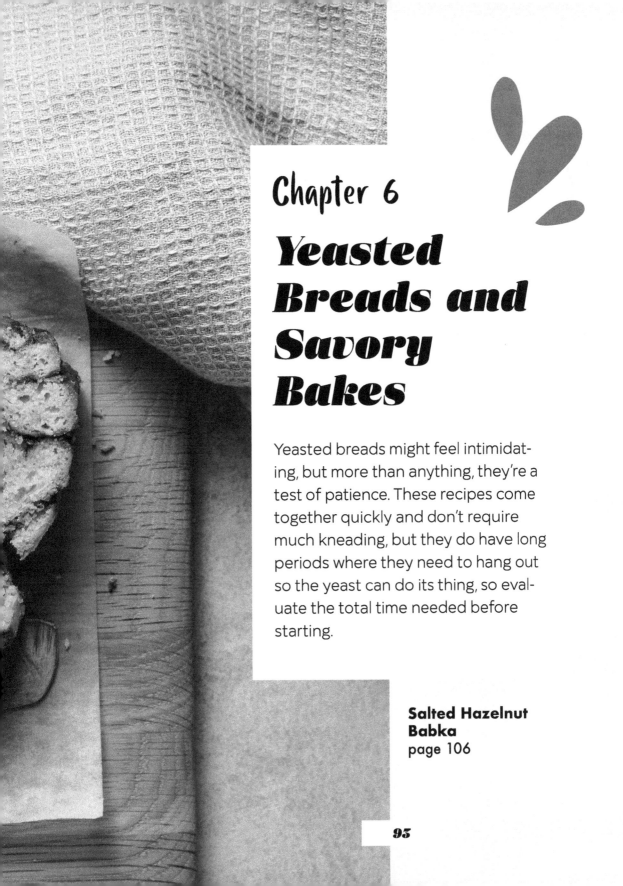

Chapter 6

Yeasted Breads and Savory Bakes

Yeasted breads might feel intimidating, but more than anything, they're a test of patience. These recipes come together quickly and don't require much kneading, but they do have long periods where they need to hang out so the yeast can do its thing, so evaluate the total time needed before starting.

Salted Hazelnut Babka
page 106

Buffalo Chicken Breadsticks

Serves 8

Prep time: 30 minutes, plus 30 minutes to rise   **Bake time:** 15 to 20 minutes

These breadsticks are the best of everything in the snacky world: soft breadsticks, Buffalo chicken, and melty cheese. It's like all the deliciousness of Buffalo dip but instead of dipping into it, it's spread onto some super fresh, soft breadsticks. I love to take a pan of these anytime our friends get together. But let's get real, some nights are ripe for snacking, and we eat these for dinner (with a side of celery, of course; we're not complete monsters).

Nonstick cooking spray

¾ cup warm water

2¼ teaspoons active
   dry yeast

1½ teaspoons granu-
   lated sugar

2⅓ cups (280g) bread flour

3 tablespoons vegetable
   oil or olive oil

1 teaspoon salt

2 tablespoons unsalted
   butter, melted

½ (8-ounce) package
   cream cheese, at room
   temperature

1 cup (165g) shredded
   cooked chicken

¼ cup hot sauce, such as
   Frank's RedHot

2 tablespoons ranch
   dressing

1½ cups shredded cheese
   (such as pepper Jack or
   cheddar), divided

1. Spray a 9-by-13-inch baking pan with non-stick spray.

2. In a medium bowl, combine the warm water, yeast, and sugar. Set the bowl aside to allow the yeast to bloom, about 10 minutes. Once the mixture is bubbly, add the flour, oil, and salt. Use a hand mixer to combine the ingredients. The dough should come together into a ball. If it doesn't, sprinkle a tablespoon of water over the top and continue mixing until it does. Put the dough in the baking pan. Set aside while you prepare the chicken.

3. Rinse and dry the bowl. Add the butter, cream cheese and chicken. Using the mixer, combine the ingredients until the chicken is finely shredded and the cream cheese is incorporated.

4. Scrape down the sides of the bowl and add the hot sauce, ranch dressing, and ½ cup cheese. Mix until fully combined.

5. Depending on the temperature of your kitchen, you might be able to stretch the dough with your hands so it covers the bottom of the baking pan. If your kitchen is cool, you might need to remove the dough from the pan and roll it out with a rolling pin to make it the right size. The dough should fit the bottom of the baking pan.

6. Cover the top of the dough with the Buffalo dip, using a spatula to spread it to the edges. Set the pan aside for 30 minutes at room temperature to allow the dough to rise slightly.

7. Meanwhile, place a rack in the lowest position in the oven. Preheat the oven to the highest setting, likely 500°F to 550°F.

8. Scatter the remaining 1 cup cheese all over the top of the Buffalo dip. Bake for 15 to 20 minutes, until thick, golden on the edges, and bubbly. Allow to cool slightly, then use a sharp knife or pizza cutter to cut four rows lengthwise and three rows crosswise.

SUBSTITUTION TIP: No need to reinvent the wheel: You can buy premade Buffalo chicken dip, so feel free to use that instead.

Lemon-Cardamom Braided Bread

Serves 12

Prep time: 25 minutes, plus 2 hours to rise **Bake time:** 30 minutes

The cardamom in this recipe pairs so beautifully with the lemon. Instead of a tart punch, they give each other a warm, aromatic hug. In this recipe, the bowl is used twice, but since the filling goes right into the dough, there's really no need to rinse it out. I work right on top of my dough crumbs.

For the dough

¾ cup milk

2 teaspoons active
  dry yeast

¼ cup (49g) granu-
  lated sugar

2 tablespoons unsalted
  butter, at room
  temperature

1 large egg

¼ teaspoon salt

3 cups (360g) all-purpose
  flour, plus more
  for dusting

1. In a Pyrex measuring cup, heat the milk in the microwave for 30 seconds, or until warm to the touch.

2. In a large bowl, combine the warm milk, yeast, and sugar. Let sit for 5 minutes, until bubbles form.

3. Add the butter, egg, salt, and flour. Using a hand mixer, mix on medium speed for 3 minutes. This is a stickier dough, so it won't form a ball. The dough should simply be consistent throughout without any lumps.

4. Cover the bowl with plastic wrap and let stand at room temperature for 1 hour 30 minutes, or until the dough is doubled in size.

5. Once the dough has risen, punch it down once or twice to knock the air out of it and knead it for about 30 seconds. Lightly dust a work surface with some flour and roll out the dough into a rectangle about 16 inches long, 12 inches wide, and ¼ inch thick, with a long side facing you. (If the dough is too sticky to work with, knead in a few table-spoons of flour. A bench scraper will help you get the dough that's stuck to your work surface.)

For the filling

½ cup (99g) granu-
lated sugar
Grated zest of 1 lemon
(about 1 tablespoon)
½ teaspoon ground
cardamom
5 tablespoons (71g)
unsalted butter,
melted, divided

6. Line a rimmed baking sheet with parchment paper.

7. To make the filling, in the same bowl, combine the sugar, lemon zest, cardamom, and 3 tablespoons butter to form a dryish paste. Cover the dough with the lemon-cardamom mixture. Starting on the longer side of the rectangle, roll the dough into a log as if you were making a cinnamon roll.

8. Cut the log lengthwise, right down the middle, so that the filling is exposed. Take the two pieces and twist them into a loose braid. On the baking sheet, roll the braid into a bun shape, tucking the loose ends under the bottom. Brush with the remaining 2 tablespoons butter. Set aside to rise, lightly covered with a kitchen towel, for 30 minutes.

9. Meanwhile, preheat the oven to 350°F.

10. Bake for 30 minutes, or until golden brown on top and bottom. Cool before slicing and serving.

Hash Brown Quiche

Serves 8

Prep time: 20 minutes   **Bake time:** 30 minutes

I'll let you in on a secret: I've never been a huge fan of quiche. I can make scrambled eggs quicker, and quiche just seems fussy. But this quiche has an irresistible crunchy hash brown crust, enough bacon to be delicious, and just enough veggies to feel like a meal. Hit it with a few splashes of your favorite hot sauce (Crystal, in my case) and you've got breakfast, brunch, or dinner.

Gluten-free nonstick cooking spray

1 cup (160g) diced bacon

1 small shallot, diced

1 garlic clove, minced

1 cup (125g) chopped broccoli

1 teaspoon dried thyme

1 teaspoon dried rosemary

Salt

Freshly ground black pepper

3½ cups (about 460g) frozen hash browns, thawed (see Ingredient tip)

½ cup heavy (whipping) cream

6 large eggs

½ cup shredded cheese (such as cheddar or pepper Jack)

1. Preheat the oven to 350°F. Coat a 9-inch pie plate with nonstick spray.

2. In a large skillet, cook the diced bacon over medium heat until crispy, about 5 minutes, stirring frequently. Carefully drain off all but 1 to 2 teaspoons of the drippings, leaving the bacon in the pan.

3. Add the shallot and sauté until soft, 1 to 2 minutes. Add the garlic and broccoli and sauté until the garlic is fragrant and the broccoli begins to turn bright green, 3 to 5 minutes. Add the thyme and rosemary and season with salt and pepper to taste. Remove the skillet from the heat and set aside to cool.

4. While the pan cools, prepare the crust. Cover the entire pie pan with the hash browns, gently squishing them together. It won't be perfect, so the egg mixture will seep through, but that's okay. The goal is to just have a layer on the bottom and up the sides of the pan.

5. Add the heavy cream to the bacon and broccoli mixture, which will help cool the pan down more before adding the eggs. The mixture should be at room temperature before you add the eggs.

6. Add the eggs and cheese and stir until fully incorporated. Season with more salt and pepper if desired. Pour the mixture into the hash brown crust.

7. Bake for 30 minutes, or until the eggs are completely set and the edges of the hash browns are crispy.

8. Serve warm. Store leftovers in an airtight container in the refrigerator for up to 3 days.

INGREDIENT TIP: You can use Tater Tots, whole or cut in half, instead of hash browns. I call for 3½ cups, but use as much or as little as you need to cover the bottom and sides of the pan. Most hash browns are gluten-free, but check the label if this is a concern.

Stuffed-Crust Pepperoni Pizza

Serves 8

Prep time: 20 minutes, plus 1 hour to rise   **Bake time:** 10 minutes

To me, pizza = party. I'm sure it's something ingrained from my childhood. But these days, you don't have to wait for an A on your report card—or, er, a perfect performance review—to celebrate with a slice. This pizza crust comes together quickly and is super easy to work with. Make it for a dinner date, movie night with friends, or just a party-o'-one.

1 tablespoon active
dry yeast

2 teaspoons granulated
sugar

1 cup warm water

3 cups (360g) bread flour,
plus more for dusting

1 teaspoon salt

½ teaspoon garlic powder

½ teaspoon Italian
seasoning

3 tablespoons olive oil

Cornmeal, for dusting

1 (8-ounce) package
mozzarella pearls

1 cup tomato or pizza
sauce of your choice

½ cup sliced pepperoni

2 cups shredded
mozzarella cheese

1. In a medium bowl, combine the yeast, sugar, and warm water. Let sit for 5 minutes, until bubbles form.

2. Add the flour, salt, garlic powder, Italian seasoning, and olive oil. Using a hand mixer on low speed, mix until just combined. Increase the speed to medium and mix until the dough forms a ball.

3. Cover the bowl with plastic wrap or a clean kitchen towel and let rest in a warm spot until the dough doubles in volume, about 1 hour.

4. While the dough rises, place a rack in the lowest position in the oven. If you have a pizza stone, put it on the lowest rack now. Preheat the oven to the highest setting, likely 500°F to 550°F.

5. Lightly dust a work surface with some flour. Once the dough has doubled in volume, scrape the dough onto it and, using a rolling pin, roll the dough into a 14-inch circle. Dust a pizza peel or pizza pan with cornmeal and transfer the dough to the peel or pan. Place the mozzarella balls about 1 inch in from the edge of the dough, forming a ring. Roll the crust over the cheese and press to seal, working all around the pizza.

**4 tablespoons
(½ stick, 56g) unsalted
butter, melted**
½ teaspoon garlic salt
**2 tablespoons grated
Parmesan cheese**
**Hot honey, for drizzling
(I like Mike's Hot Honey)**

6. Use a spoon to spread the tomato sauce all over the dough, followed by the pepperoni and shredded cheese. In the bowl used to make the dough, combine the melted butter, garlic salt, and Parmesan. Brush the edges of the crust with the Parmesan butter. (Keep the rest for dipping.)

7. Transfer the pizza from the peel to the pizza stone or place the pizza pan on the lowest rack. Bake the pizza for about 10 minutes, until the cheese is bubbly and the edges are golden brown. Drizzle a bit of the hot honey over each slice before serving.

Everything Brown Bread

Makes 2 medium loaves

Prep time: 20 minutes, plus 1 hour 30 minutes to rise   **Bake time:** 25 minutes

There's not much better in this world than a piece of warm bread slathered with butter. This brown bread gets its color from cocoa, dark brown sugar, and molasses, but it manages to still be savory with just a hint of sweetness. The everything seasoning gives it a multitude of flavors with a satisfying crunch. Bake this up and impress your friends with your baking prowess—just don't tell them you did it all with just one bowl.

1½ cups warm water

1 tablespoon active
   dry yeast

2 tablespoons dark
   brown sugar

1 tablespoon
   Dutch-process
   cocoa powder

¼ cup molasses

2 teaspoons salt

2 cups (240g)
   whole-wheat flour

1½ cups (180g) bread flour

2 tablespoons vege-
   table oil

3 tablespoons everything
   bagel seasoning

1. In a medium bowl, combine the warm water, yeast, and brown sugar and stir to combine. Allow the yeast to bloom for 5 minutes, until it's foamy.

2. Add the cocoa, molasses, salt, and whole-wheat flour. Use a hand mixer (fitted with dough hooks, if it has them) and mix to combine. Add the bread flour and mix until well combined. The dough should come together into a rough ball.

3. Pour the oil over the top of the dough. Knead the dough in the bowl for about 1 minute. The oil should coat the dough as well as get mixed in. Shape the dough into a ball and cover the bowl with plastic wrap. Place the bowl in a warm spot and allow the dough to rise for 1 hour, or until it has doubled in volume.

4. While the dough is rising, line a rimmed baking sheet with parchment paper.

5. Once the dough has doubled in volume, turn it out onto a clean work surface. The oil should keep it from sticking. Divide the dough in half. Knead one half a few times, then shape it into a 3-by-6-inch loaf, carefully tucking the edges underneath. Repeat with the second loaf. Place the loaves side by side on the baking sheet. Cover the top of the loaves with the everything bagel seasoning.

6. Cover the loaves with a clean kitchen towel and allow the bread to rise again for 30 minutes.

7. Meanwhile, preheat the oven to 350°F.

8. Bake the loaves for 25 minutes. When finished, the loaves will be dark brown with a golden bottom and should move freely on the baking sheet. The loaves should have a hollow sound when the bottoms are tapped. The center will be slightly dense and chewy. Serve warm.

Cheater's Kolaches

Makes 8 kolaches

Prep time: 30 minutes, plus 1 hour 30 minutes to rise   **Bake time:** 15 minutes

Some people call kolaches the new doughnut, while others consider them to be similar to a Danish. This Czech pastry has a cult-like following in Texas, and for good reason. It is a pillowy soft bread topped with fresh fruit or (in this case) a cream cheese topping and dusting of streusel. Now we really can't cheat our way out of the dough, but the filling and the streusel? I have a way to work around that.

1 cup milk

½ cup granulated sugar

1 tablespoon active
    dry yeast

4 tablespoons (½ stick,
    56g) unsalted butter, at
    room temperature, plus
    2 tablespoons unsalted
    butter, melted

1 large egg

1 large egg yolk

1 teaspoon salt

3 cups (360g) bread flour

3 tablespoons honey

¼ teaspoon ground
    cinnamon

1 (8-ounce) container
    whipped cream cheese

2 tablespoons graham
    cracker crumbs (or 2 to
    3 crumbled cookies, such
    as Biscoff)

1. In a Pyrex measuring cup, heat the milk in the microwave for 30 seconds, or until warm to the touch.

2. In a medium bowl, combine the warm milk, sugar, and yeast. Allow the yeast to bubble for about 5 minutes.

3. Add the room-temperature butter, egg, egg yolk, salt, and 1 cup flour. Using a hand mixer on low, mix until combined. Add the remaining 2 cups flour and mix on low until the dough starts to come together. Increase the speed to high and mix for 1 to 2 minutes, until the dough starts to form a ball and make its way up the beaters.

4. Knead the dough into a ball. Cover the bowl with plastic wrap or a clean kitchen towel. Allow it to rest somewhere warm for 1 hour, or until the dough doubles in volume.

5. While the dough is rising, stir the honey and cinnamon into the cream cheese right in the container it came in. Line a rimmed baking sheet with parchment paper.

6. Once the dough has risen, divide it in half. Divide each half into four portions, for eight portions total.

7. Roll a dough portion into a ball in your hand, working to tuck the edges underneath until you have a ball that is smooth on the top and sides. Place it on the baking sheet. Repeat this process with the remaining dough. Cover with a kitchen towel and allow the dough to rise for another 30 minutes.

8. Preheat the oven to 400°F.

9. Using the bottom of a ¼-cup measuring cup, press an indentation into each ball of dough. Brush the dough with the melted butter, then fill it with 1 to 2 tablespoons cream cheese filling (or as much as you like). Top with the graham cracker crumbs.

10. Bake for 15 minutes, or until the tops are golden brown.

SUBSTITUTION TIP: The crumble on top is key. Every time I get a toasty, crunchy bit, it sends that bite over the top. So don't skip it. But do dig around in the pantry and get creative. I tried several things: Vanilla wafers? Yes. Crunchy chocolate chip cookies? Yes. Ritz crackers? Where have you been all my life?

VARIATION TIP: These end up a good-size treat, 3½ to 4 inches in diameter after they are baked. You can also divide the dough more to make them smaller. Ten would still produce a nice treat, while a dozen would qualify as mini. If making smaller sizes, you'll need to reduce the baking time slightly.

Salted Hazelnut Babka

Makes 1 large loaf

Prep time: 20 minutes, plus 3 hours to rise   **Bake time:** 35 to 40 minutes

Can we all agree that "babka" is just fun to say? I am, of course, familiar with this classic Jewish baked good because of Seinfeld. *In one episode, there's the chocolate babka and then the "lesser babka," the cinnamon one. In my view, there is even a superior babka, the salted hazelnut babka. The salt intensifies the chocolate-hazelnut spread in a way you never knew was missing. This one has a long rest time, but that just means you can knock out a few episodes of* Seinfeld *while you wait.*

1 cup heavy (whipping) cream, warmed

1 tablespoon active dry yeast

½ cup (99g) granulated sugar

4 tablespoons (½ stick, 56g) unsalted butter, at room temperature

2 large eggs

3⅔ cups (440g) all-purpose flour, plus additional for dusting

½ teaspoon table salt

½ cup chocolate-hazelnut spread

1 teaspoon coarse salt, such as kosher, Maldon, or sea salt

1. Line a 10-inch loaf pan with a parchment-paper sling (see Technique tip on page 47).

2. In a large bowl, combine the warm cream, yeast, and sugar. Allow the yeast to bloom and bubble, about 5 minutes.

3. Add the butter and eggs. Using a hand mixer, mix to combine. Add the flour and table salt. The dough should be uniform with no lumps. Briefly knead the dough in the bowl to pull together any stuck bits. The dough should be wet, but not sticky. Form the dough into a ball and cover bowl with plastic wrap. Set aside in a warm place and allow to rise for 2 hours, or until the dough has doubled in volume.

4. Once the dough has doubled in volume, dust a clean work surface with some flour. Using a rolling pin, roll the dough out into a large square, about 20-by-20-inches and about ¼ inch thick. Cut it into two rectangles, with the short end facing you.

5. Using a spatula, smooth the chocolate-hazelnut spread over both dough rectangles, and sprinkle the coarse salt over the surface.

6. Starting on the short side of each rectangle, roll each up like a cinnamon roll. Cut one log down the center lengthwise, revealing all the layers. Gently "braid" these two pieces, allowing the cut portion to be seen on top. Repeat with the second log. Place both in the loaf pan, one on top of the other. Sprinkle the top with more salt.

7. Cover with a clean kitchen towel and allow the dough to rise again for 1 hour.

8. Preheat the oven to 350°F.

9. Bake the loaf for 35 to 40 minutes, until the top is brown, the hazelnut spread is crackly, and bread separates from the edges of the pan.

10. Allow to cool slightly before slicing to reveal your lovely swirls.

TECHNIQUE TIP: If you don't have a large loaf pan, your bread might try to escape. Either take your chances and place the loaf pan on a sheet pan, or only use three-quarters of the dough and make mini babkas with the remainder.

Spinach-Tomato Strata

Serves 8

Prep time: 15 minutes   **Bake time:** 1 hour 15 minutes

I love this strata because it's as beautiful as it is delicious. You can also make it ahead (just refrigerate overnight, covered, then bake in the morning), or make it even easier by chopping everything up and tossing it in a 9-by-13-inch pan (this will cut the cook time roughly in half).

9 thick slices brioche bread

2 cups baby spinach, divided

¼ cup diced oil-packed sun-dried tomatoes, divided

1 cup shredded mozzarella cheese, divided

6 large eggs

1 cup milk

½ cup heavy (whipping) cream

¼ cup grated Parmesan cheese

2 tablespoons oil from the jar of sun-dried tomatoes

1 teaspoon dried rosemary

1 teaspoon dried thyme

1 teaspoon salt

½ teaspoon freshly ground black pepper

½ teaspoon red pepper flakes

1. Preheat the oven to 375°F.

2. Trim the bread and layer 3 pieces in a 10-inch loaf pan. Top with half of the spinach, half of the sun-dried tomatoes, and one-third of the mozzarella. Repeat with 3 more slices of bread, the remaining spinach and tomatoes, and another third of the mozzarella. Finish with the remaining bread and mozzarella.

3. In a medium bowl, whisk the eggs, milk, cream, Parmesan, sun-dried tomato oil, rosemary, thyme, salt, black pepper, and red pepper flakes.

4. Pour the egg mixture over the loaf pan, working in batches, to let the bread soak it up. Tightly cover the pan with aluminum foil.

5. Bake for 45 minutes. Remove the foil and bake for about 30 minutes more. The top will be golden, and it should feel firm when pressed. Serve warm.

Beef Potpie Pockets

Serves 6

Prep time: 25 minutes   **Bake time:** 15 minutes

These pockets pack all the flavor of a beef potpie in a flaky crust. You can prep the pies and freeze them before baking; when that craving for comfort food hits, just thaw one slightly in the microwave and bake as directed.

¼ cup diced onions

2 tablespoons olive oil

7 ounces (200g)
   80-percent lean
   ground beef

½ teaspoon garlic powder

½ teaspoon onion powder

Salt

Freshly ground
   black pepper

1 tablespoon
   all-purpose flour

¼ cup beef broth

1½ cups mixed vegeta-
   bles (I like a mixture of
   potato, carrot, peas, and
   green beans), drained
   if canned or thawed
   if frozen

1 (17.3-ounce) package
   puff pastry, thawed
   in the refrigerator
   overnight

1 large egg, beaten

1. Preheat the oven to 400°F. Line a rimmed baking sheet with parchment paper.

2. In a large skillet over medium-high heat, sauté the onions in the olive oil until translucent, 3 to 5 minutes. Add the ground beef, breaking it up with a spoon. Add the garlic powder and onion powder and season with salt and pepper. Cook, stirring often, until the meat is cooked through, 5 to 7 minutes. Sprinkle the flour over the top and stir to combine. Add the broth; stir until it thickens. Stir in the mixed vegetables and set aside.

3. Lay one piece of puff pastry on a clean workspace and cut it into six equal squares or rectangles, depending your puff pastry sheets. Space them out on the baking sheet, and divide the beef mixture between the center of these six pieces. Cut the second sheet of puff pastry to match.

4. Brush the edges of the pastry with the beaten egg. Place a second piece of puff pastry on top of each, gently stretching it to cover the beef. Use a fork to crimp the edges to seal them. Brush the tops with more of the beaten egg.

5. Bake for 15 minutes, or until the tops are golden brown. The bottom should be brown as well. Let rest for a few minutes before serving.

Citrus-Cherry Milk Bread

Makes 1 large boule

Prep time: 20 minutes, plus 3 hours to rise   **Bake time:** 25 to 30 minutes

This bread is a case study in texture and flavor. The outside is crunchy, while the inside is moist and sweet, studded with tart dried cherries that have rehydrated. The whole loaf is scented with orange and lemon. It's pillowy perfection, only to be elevated by a smear of honey butter. The base starts with a tangzhong, the traditional starter of Japanese milk bread. It's a flour and water slurry that adds moisture, creating a softer bread with a longer shelf life. I have, of course, adjusted the method to fit just one bowl.

For the tangzhong

⅓ **cup milk**
⅓ **cup water**
2 **tablespoons
    all-purpose flour**

For the bread

½ **cup milk**
2¼ **teaspoons active
    dry yeast**
½ **cup (99g) granu-
    lated sugar**
4 **tablespoons (½ stick,
    56g) unsalted butter, at
    room temperature, plus
    1 tablespoon, melted, for
    brushing**
1 **large egg**
1 **large egg yolk**

1. To make the tangzhong, in a medium microwave-safe bowl, whisk together the milk, water, and flour to combine. Microwave for 3 minutes, stopping and whisking the mixture every minute. It will become thicker and slightly gooey. Place in the refrigerator to cool for about 5 minutes while you gather the rest of your ingredients.

2. To make the bread, in a Pyrex measuring cup, heat the milk in the microwave for 30 seconds, or until warm to the touch.

3. Add the milk, yeast, and sugar to the tangzhong. Stir gently to combine. Allow the yeast to begin to bubble, about 5 minutes.

4. Once the yeast is bubbling, add the butter, egg, and egg yolk. Using a hand mixer, combine with the tangzhong. Add 3 cups flour and the salt. Mix to combine until the dough is uniform throughout. Mix in the cherries, lemon zest, and orange zest until incorporated and uniform.

3 ⅓ cups (400g)
  all-purpose flour,
  divided, plus additional
  for dusting
½ teaspoon salt
½ cup (4 ounces, 113g)
  dried tart cherries
Grated zest of 1 lemon
Grated zest of 1 orange

5. Sprinkle the remaining ⅓ cup flour over the top and knead it into the dough by hand, for no more than 1 minute. Shape the dough into a ball. Cover the bowl with a clean kitchen towel. Set aside in a warm place to proof for 2 hours, or until the dough has doubled in volume.

6. Line a rimmed baking sheet with parchment paper. Punch down the dough. Lightly dust a clean work surface with flour and briefly knead for 30 seconds to 1 minute. Shape it into a large, round loaf and place on the baking sheet.

7. Brush the surface with melted butter. If you're feeling fancy, use a sharp knife to cut a small design into the top. Set aside to rise again, uncovered, for 1 hour.

8. Preheat the oven to 350°F.

9. Bake for 25 to 30 minutes, until the top is golden and the bread sounds hollow when you tap it on the bottom.

VARIATION TIP: You can also divide the dough into 12 portions and form them into rolls. These would be a wonderful addition to an Easter brunch or just to have for easy snacking. Bake for 15 minutes, then check for doneness.

Measurement Conversions

VOLUME EQUIVALENTS		U.S. Standard	U.S. Standard (ounces)	Metric (approximate)
LIQUID		2 tablespoons	1 fl. oz.	30 mL
		¼ cup	2 fl. oz.	60 mL
		½ cup	4 fl. oz.	120 mL
		1 cup	8 fl. oz.	240 mL
		1½ cups	12 fl. oz.	355 mL
		2 cups or 1 pint	16 fl. oz.	475 mL
		4 cups or 1 quart	32 fl. oz.	1 L
		1 gallon	128 fl. oz.	4 L
DRY		⅛ teaspoon		0.5 mL
		¼ teaspoon		1 mL
		½ teaspoon		2 mL
		¾ teaspoon		4 mL
		1 teaspoon		5 mL
		1 tablespoon		15 mL
		¼ cup		59 mL
		⅓ cup		79 mL
		½ cup		118 mL
		⅔ cup		156 mL
		¾ cup		177 mL
		1 cup		235 mL
		2 cups or 1 pint		475 mL
		3 cups		700 mL
		4 cups or 1 quart		1 L
		½ gallon		2 L
		1 gallon		4 L

OVEN TEMPERATURES

Fahrenheit	Celsius (approximate)
250°F	120°C
300°F	150°C
325°F	165°C
350°F	180°C
375°F	190°C
400°F	200°C
425°F	220°C
450°F	230°C

WEIGHT EQUIVALENTS

U.S. Standard	Metric (approximate)
½ ounce	15 g
1 ounce	30 g
2 ounces	60 g
4 ounces	115 g
8 ounces	225 g
12 ounces	340 g
16 ounces or 1 pound	455 g

Index

Acknowledgments

Thank you to everyone at Callisto Media, especially my editor, Cecily McAndrews, who got all my jokes and appreciated every stupid pun and didn't complain when I could never, ever get the butter right. Thank you, Matt Buonaguro, who found me and invited me to this project after a very 2020 start. Thank you, Julie Kerr, who proved that sometimes the second time is, in fact, a charm. Thanks to Brad, who suffered through at least 150 rounds of recipe testing and all the dishes they produced. To Erin Robinson, who was always there to help push me when I needed it and reel me back in when I needed that even more! To Kyle McLaughlin, my oldest friend, for always making sure I don't look like an idiot. And to my leftovers group for helping me dispose of ALL THINGS SWEET. You guys rock. I had two books as inspiration for this book: *Delights from the Delta*, by the 1977 Chicot County Extension Homemakers Club, and *Delicious Designs*, compiled by the 1968 employees of Malouf Company. Thank you for knowing when to keep it simple.

About the Author

Kelli Marks is a self-taught cake decorator turned pastry chef. She is the owner of Sweet Love, a brick-and-mortar shop now operating as a cottage bakery specializing in wedding cakes. Her interest in baking began early under the tutelage of her grandmother. Her love of art and drawing bloomed into a hobby of creating ephemeral art through food. Her desserts have been featured in her local market in *Weddings in Arkansas*, *Arkansas Life*, *Soiree*, and *Arkansas Bride*; nationally in *Southern Living*, *Southern Bride*, and *Taste of the South*; and globally in *Eat Smarter*. Other recipes appear in *The Modern Arkansas Table*, *Another Slice of Arkansas Pie*, and *43 Tables: An Internet Community Cooks During Quarantine*. She spends any time she's not covered in frosting with her dogs, Presley and Phoebe, or on a beach with her husband, Brad.

Heather Farmer, of BostonGirlBakes.com, also contributed several cookie recipes to the book.